Space Coloring Book for Kids

Color Test Page

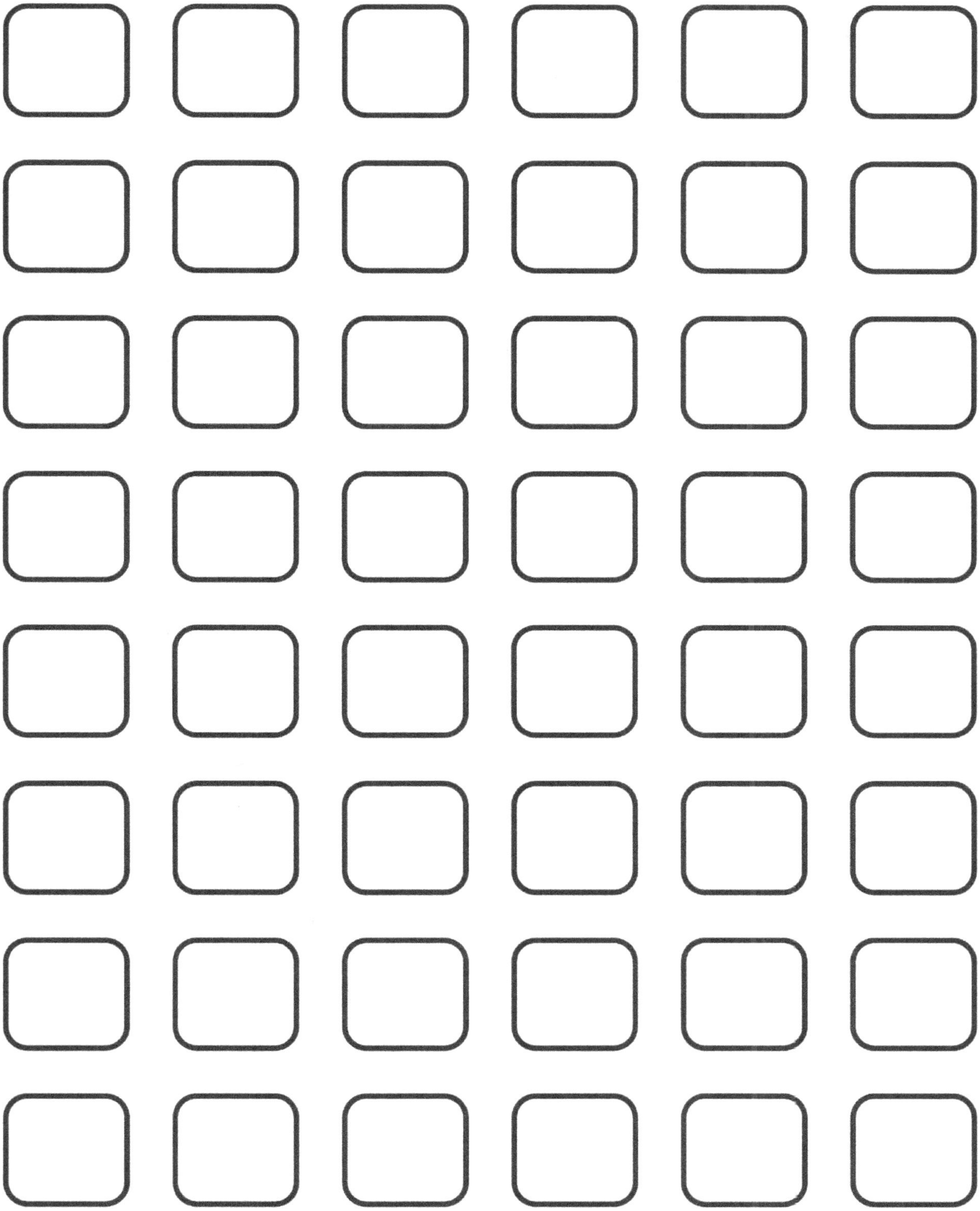

Color Test Page

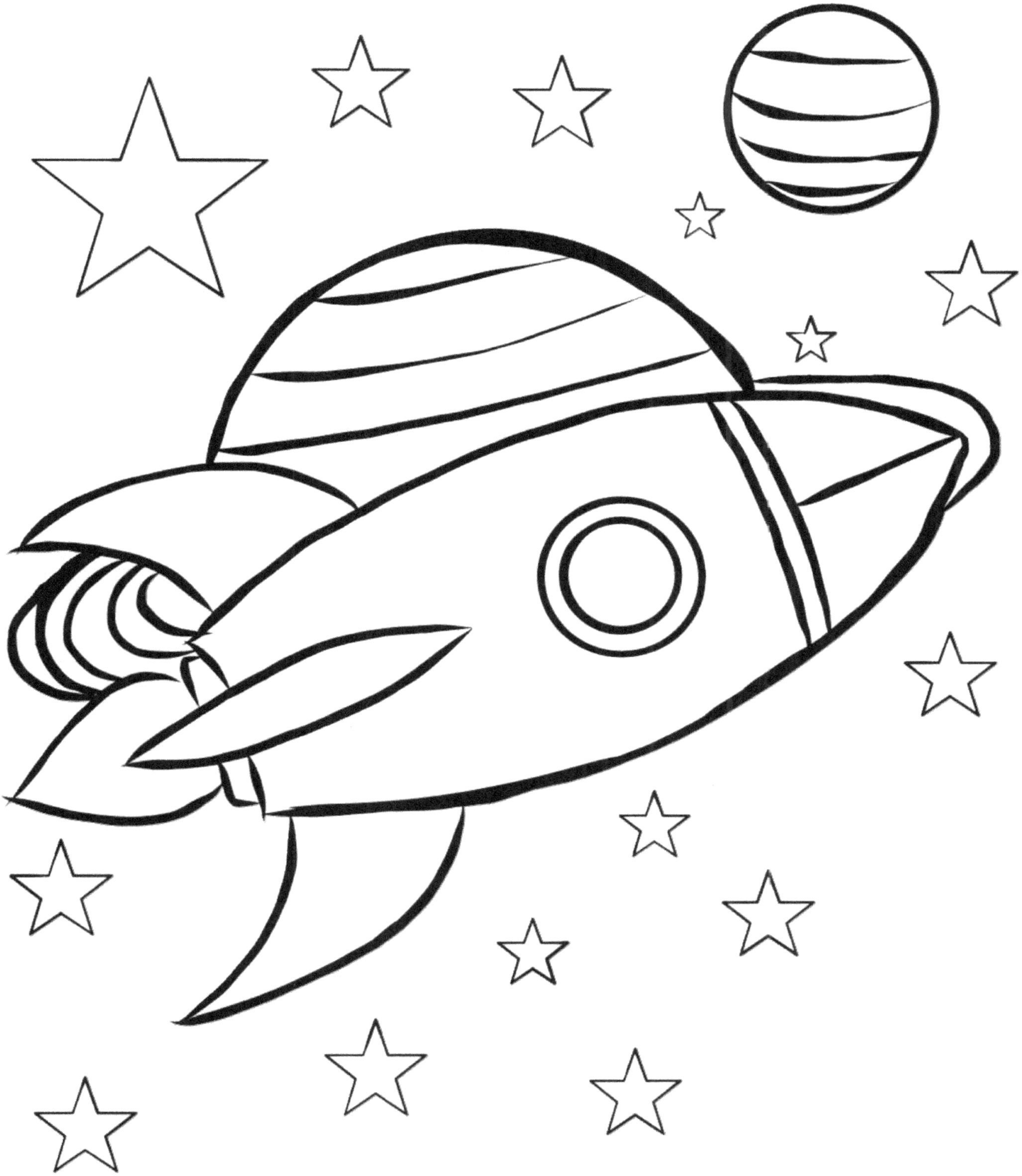

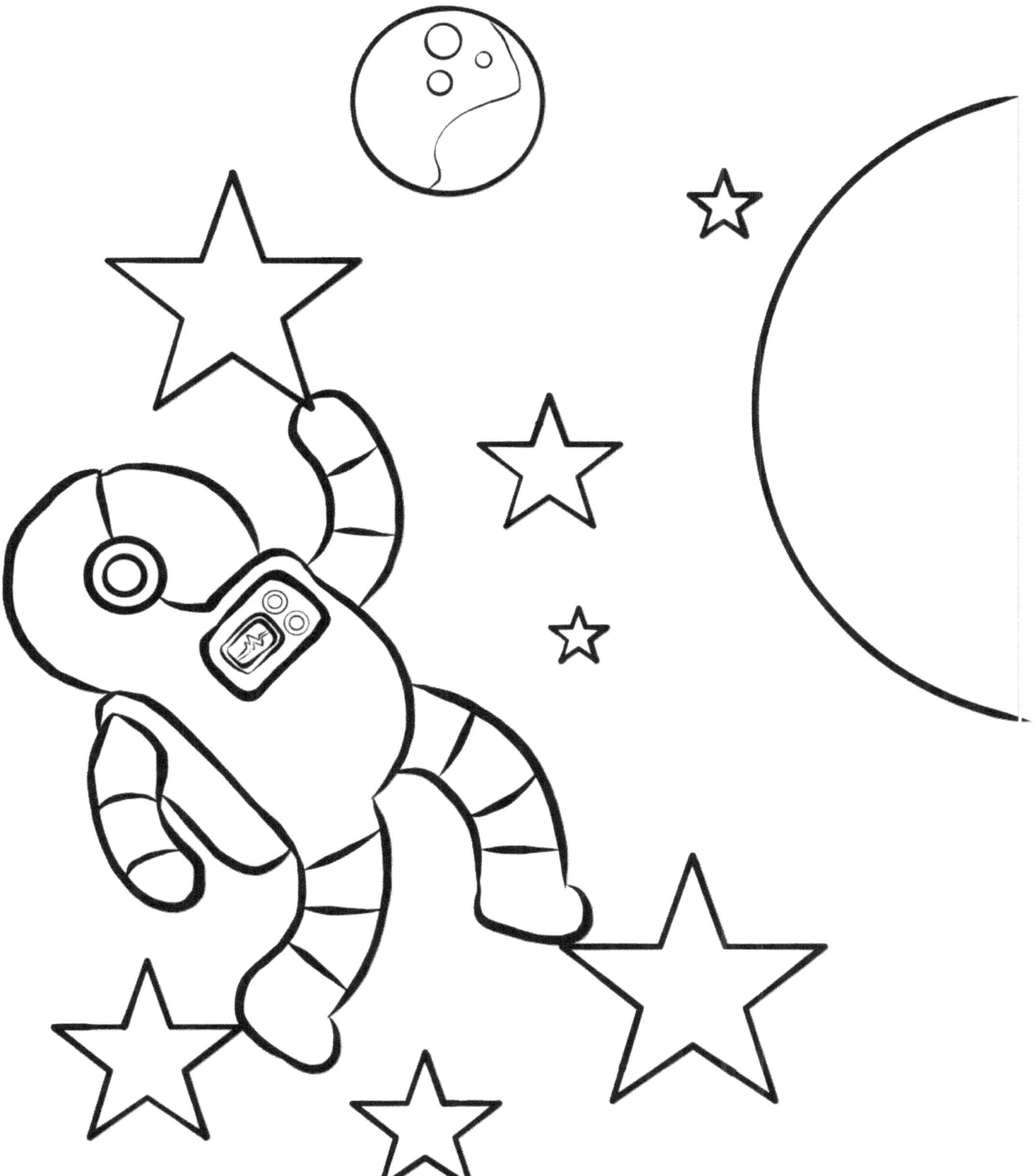

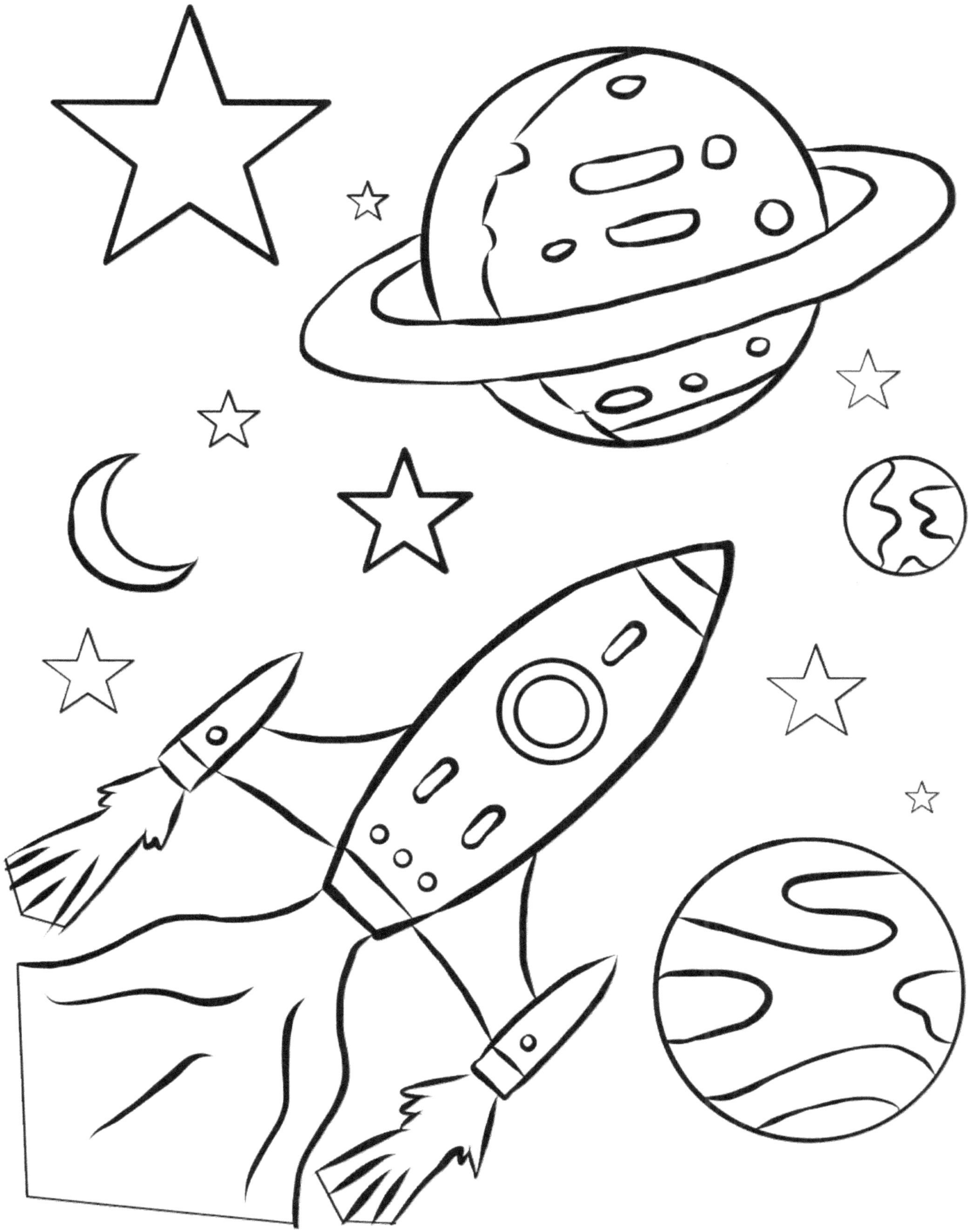

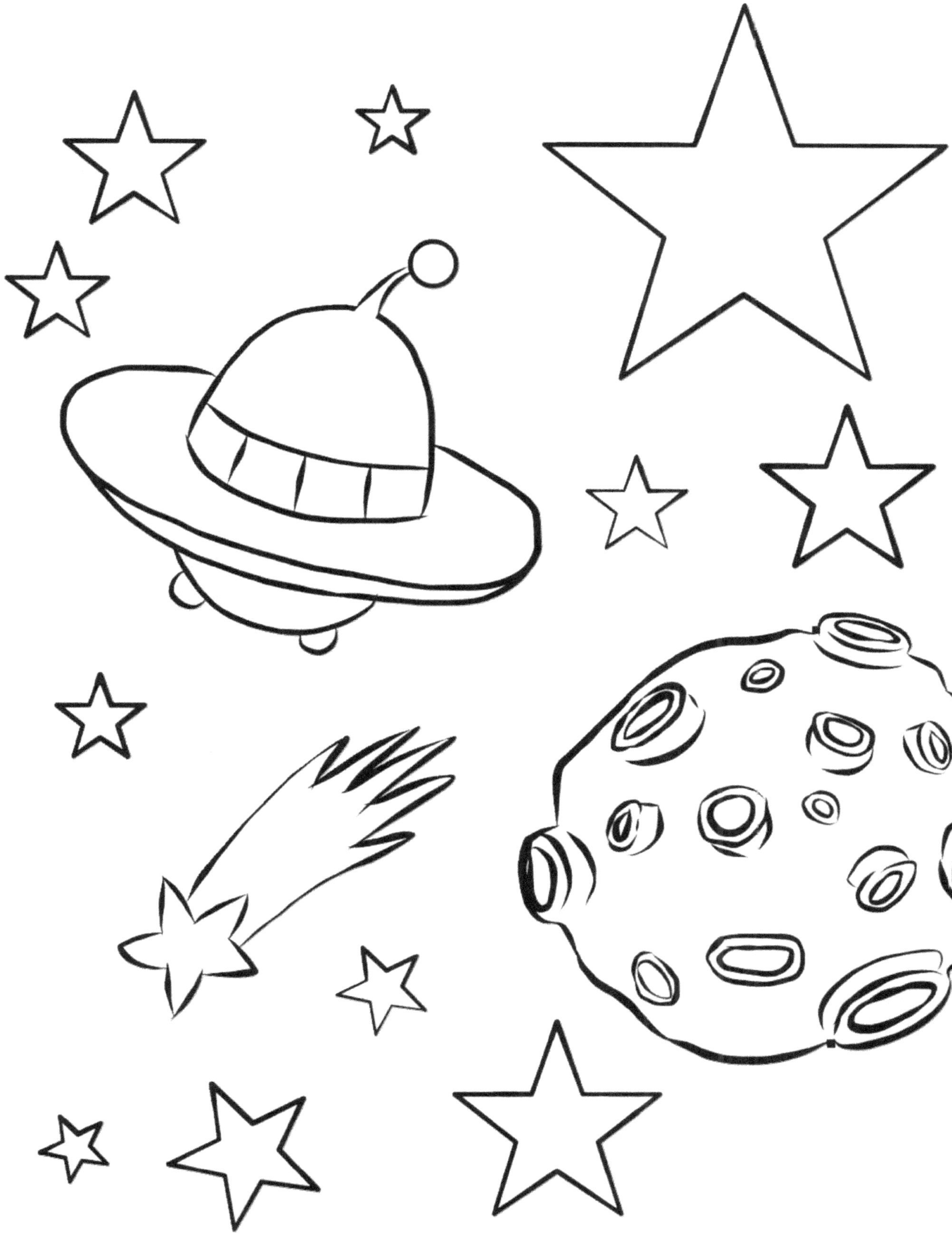

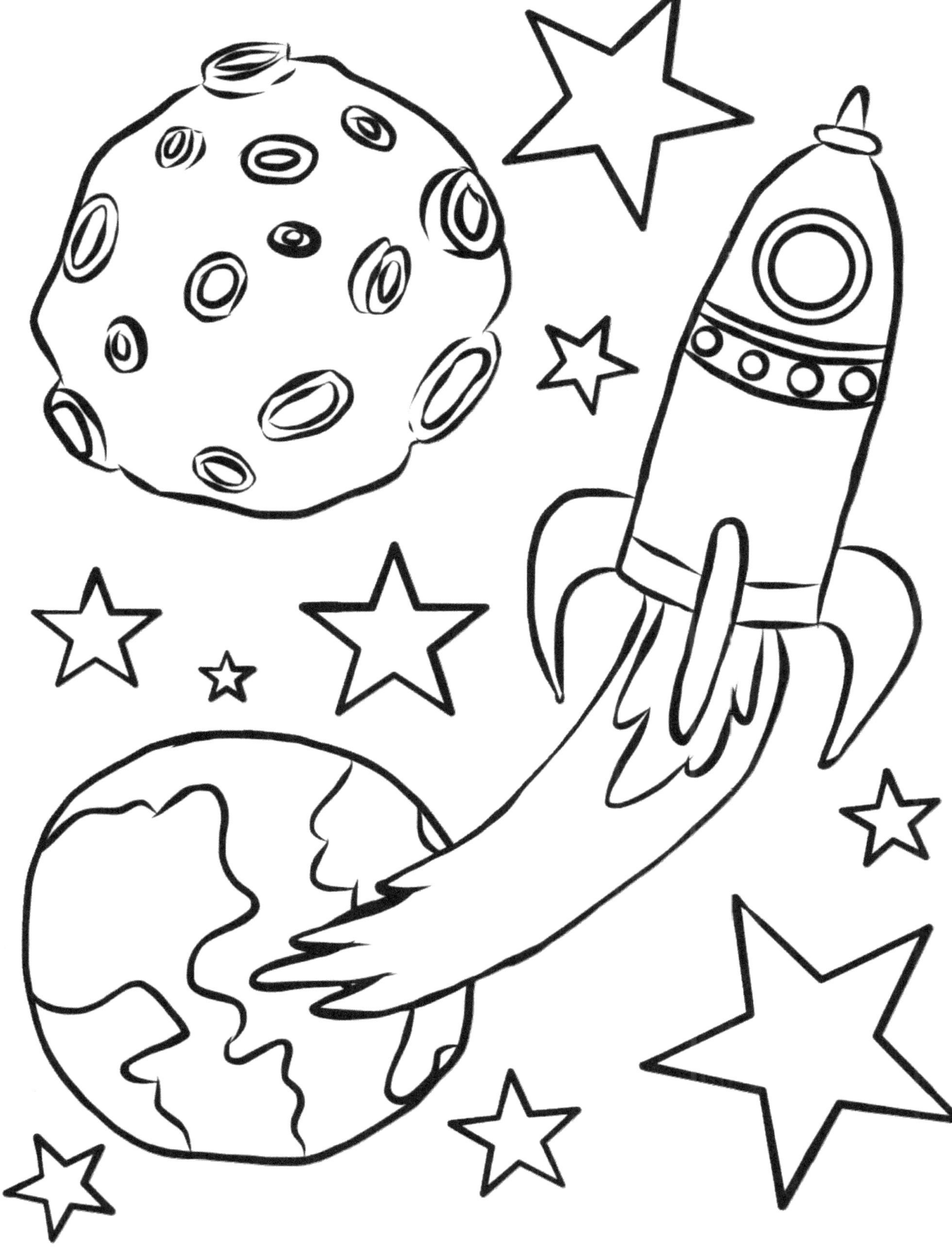

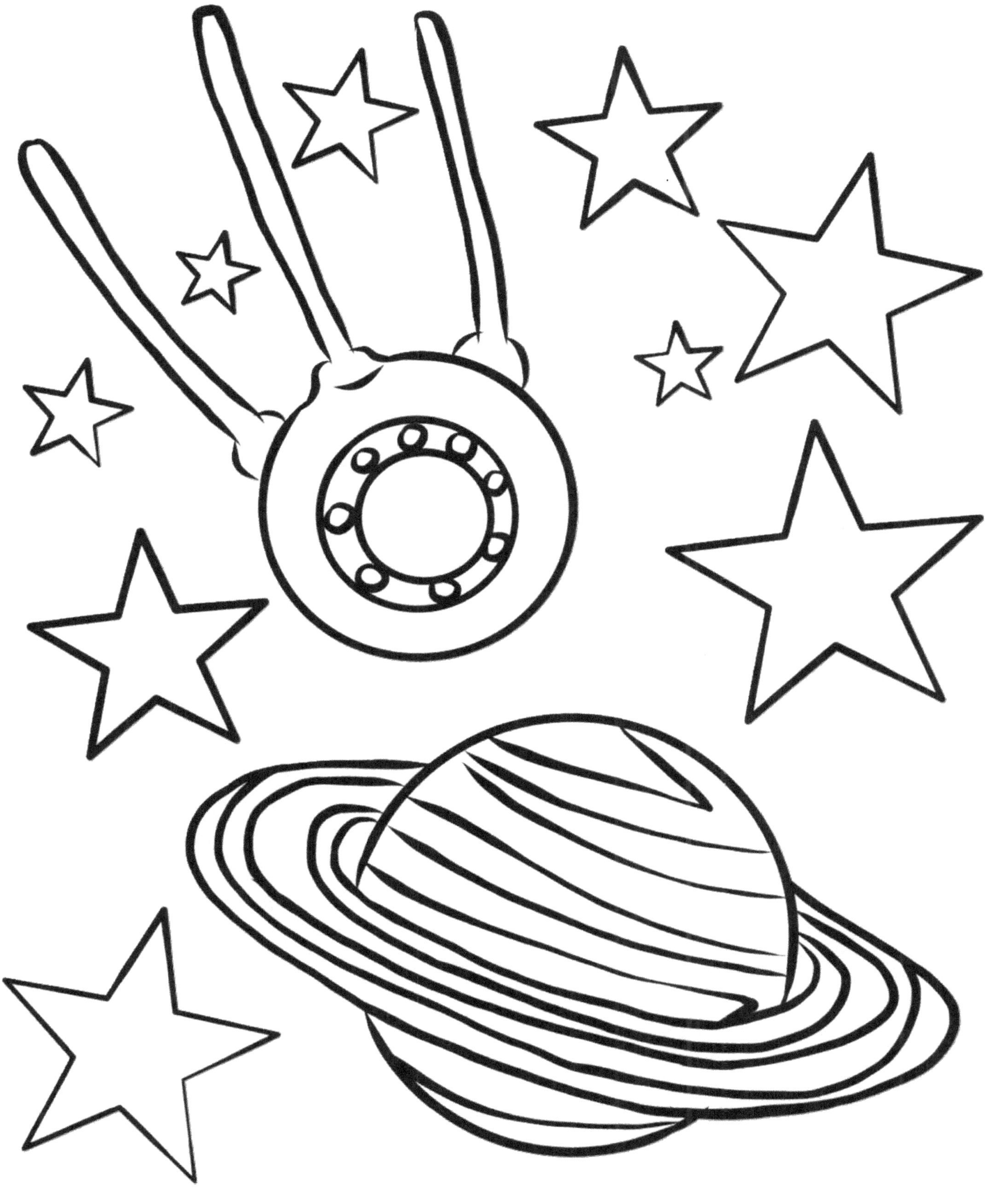

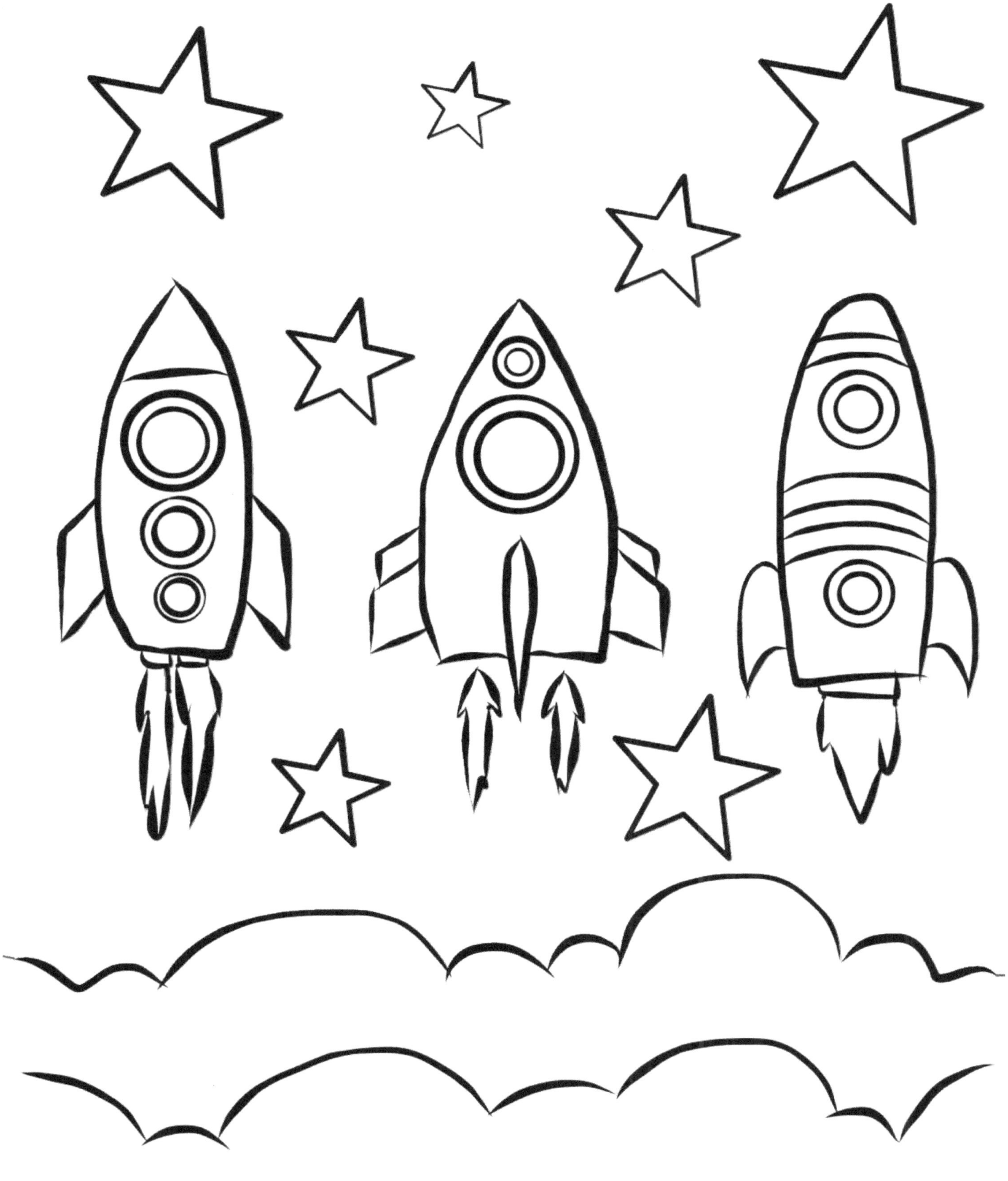

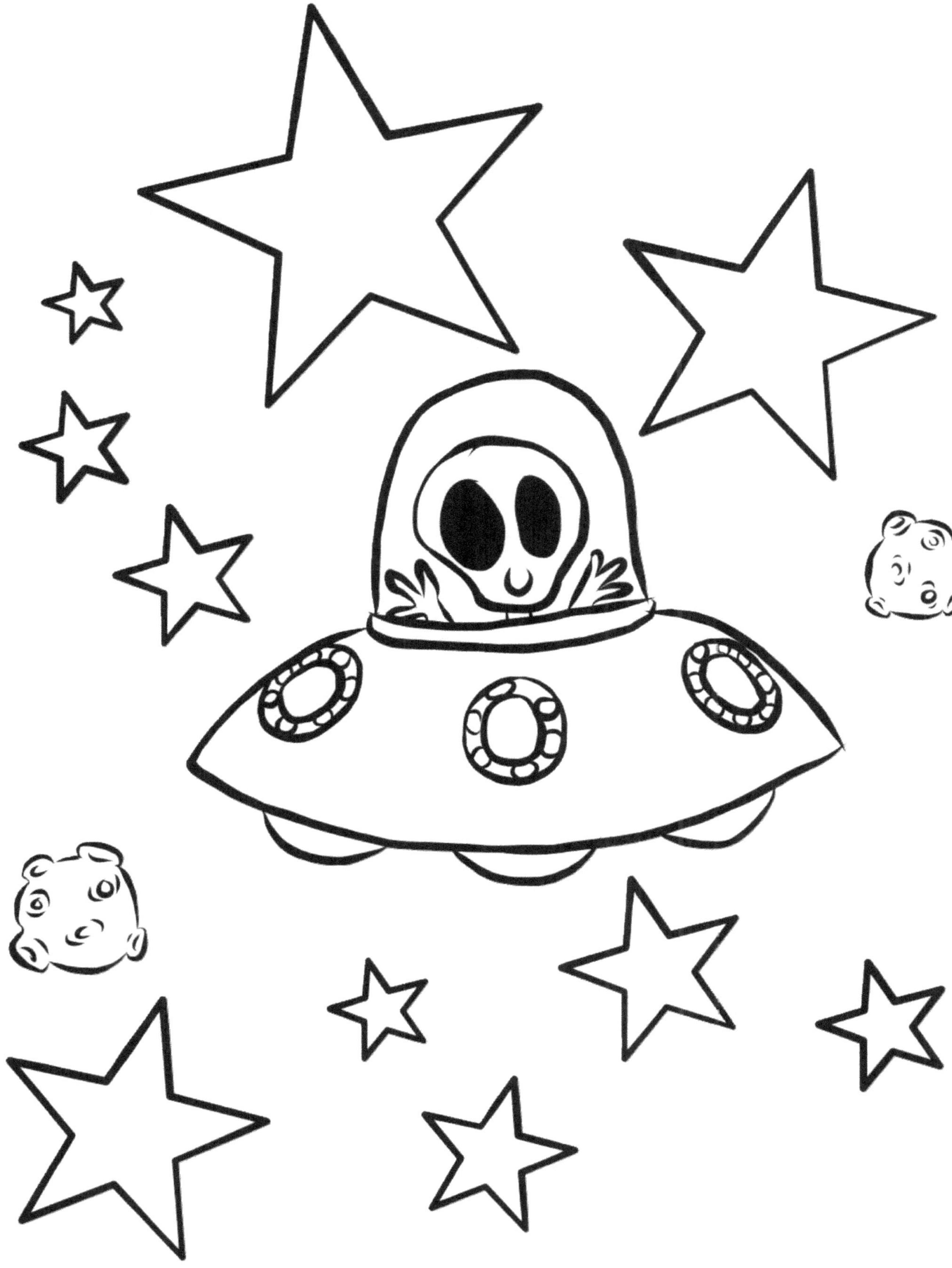

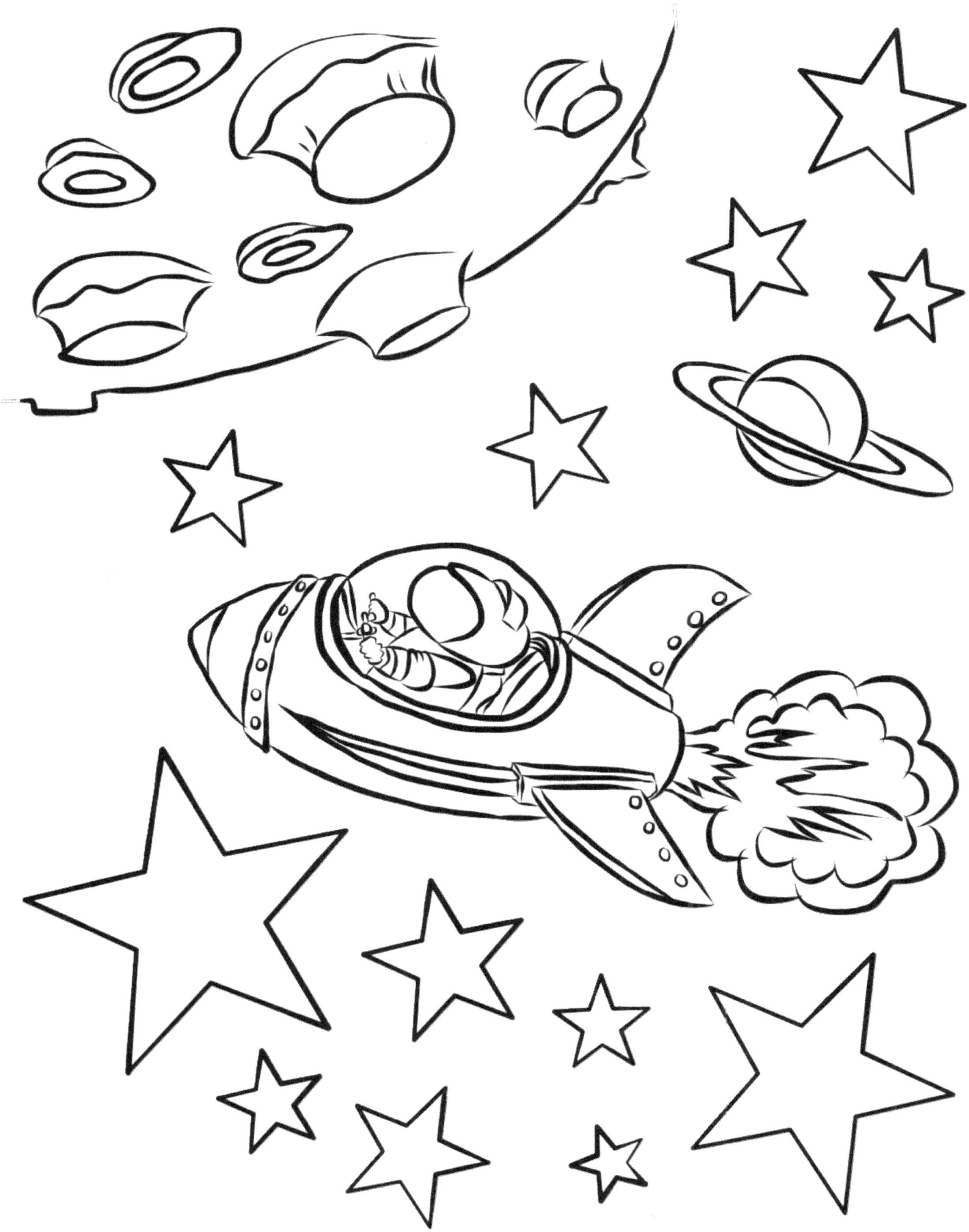

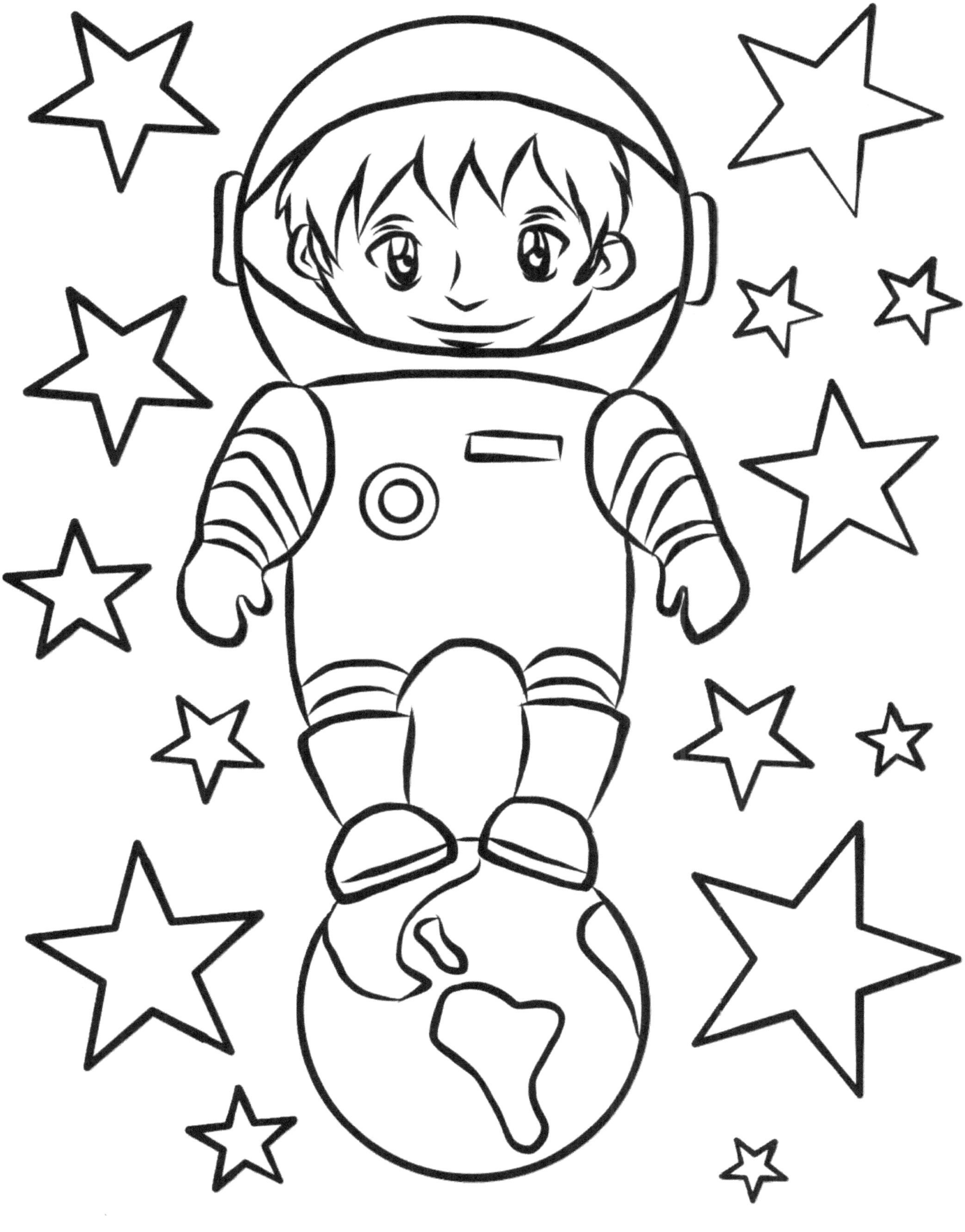

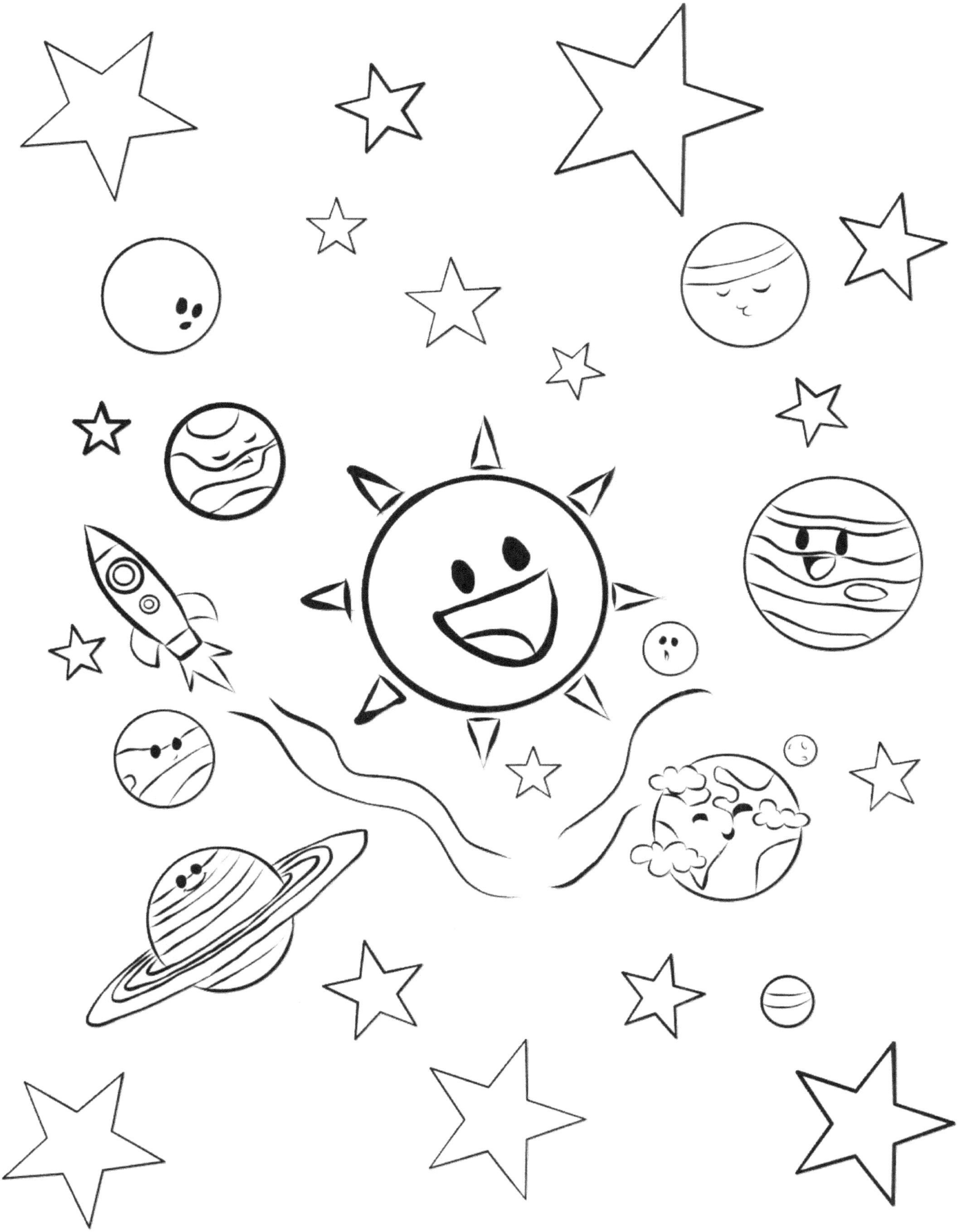

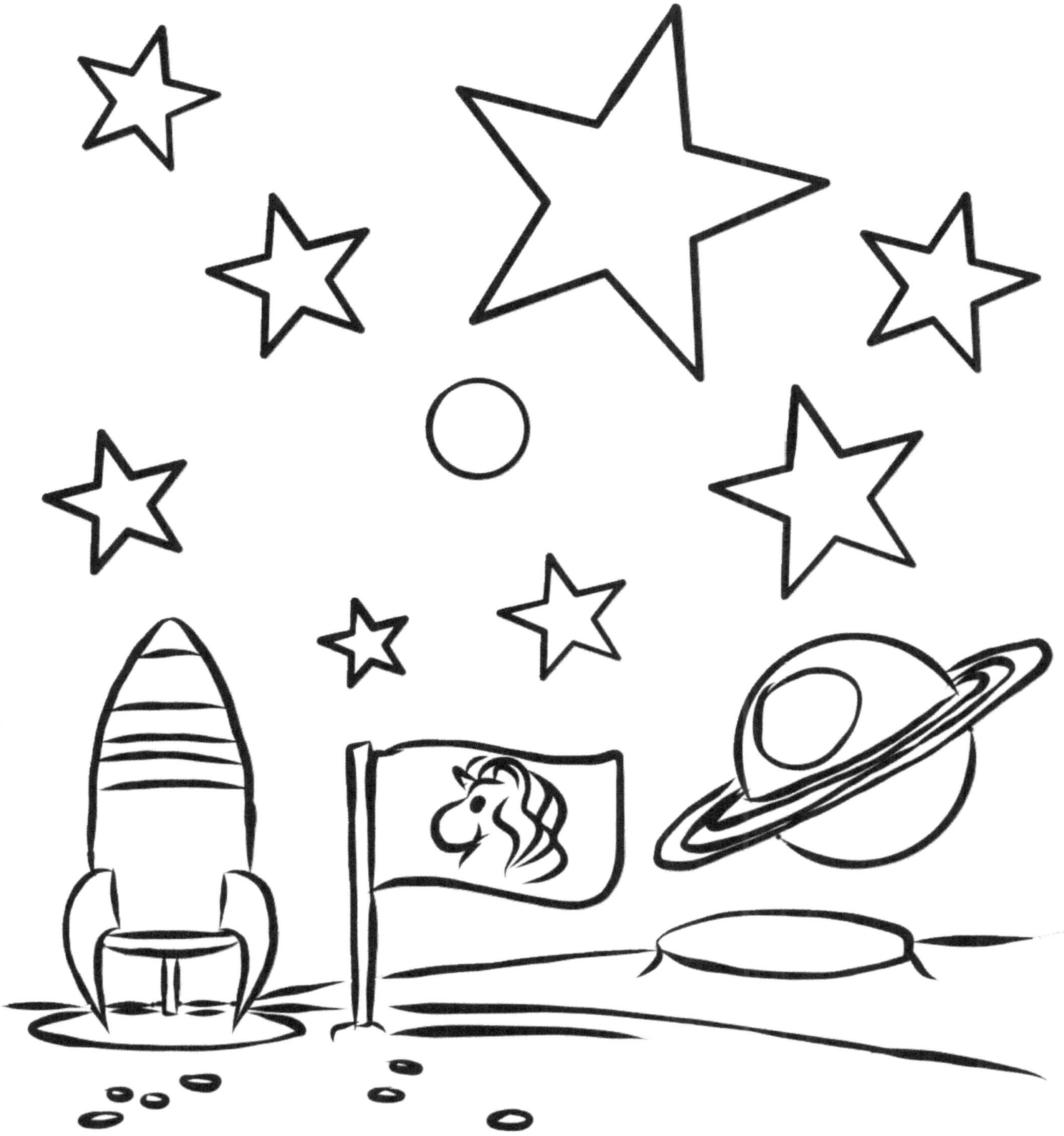

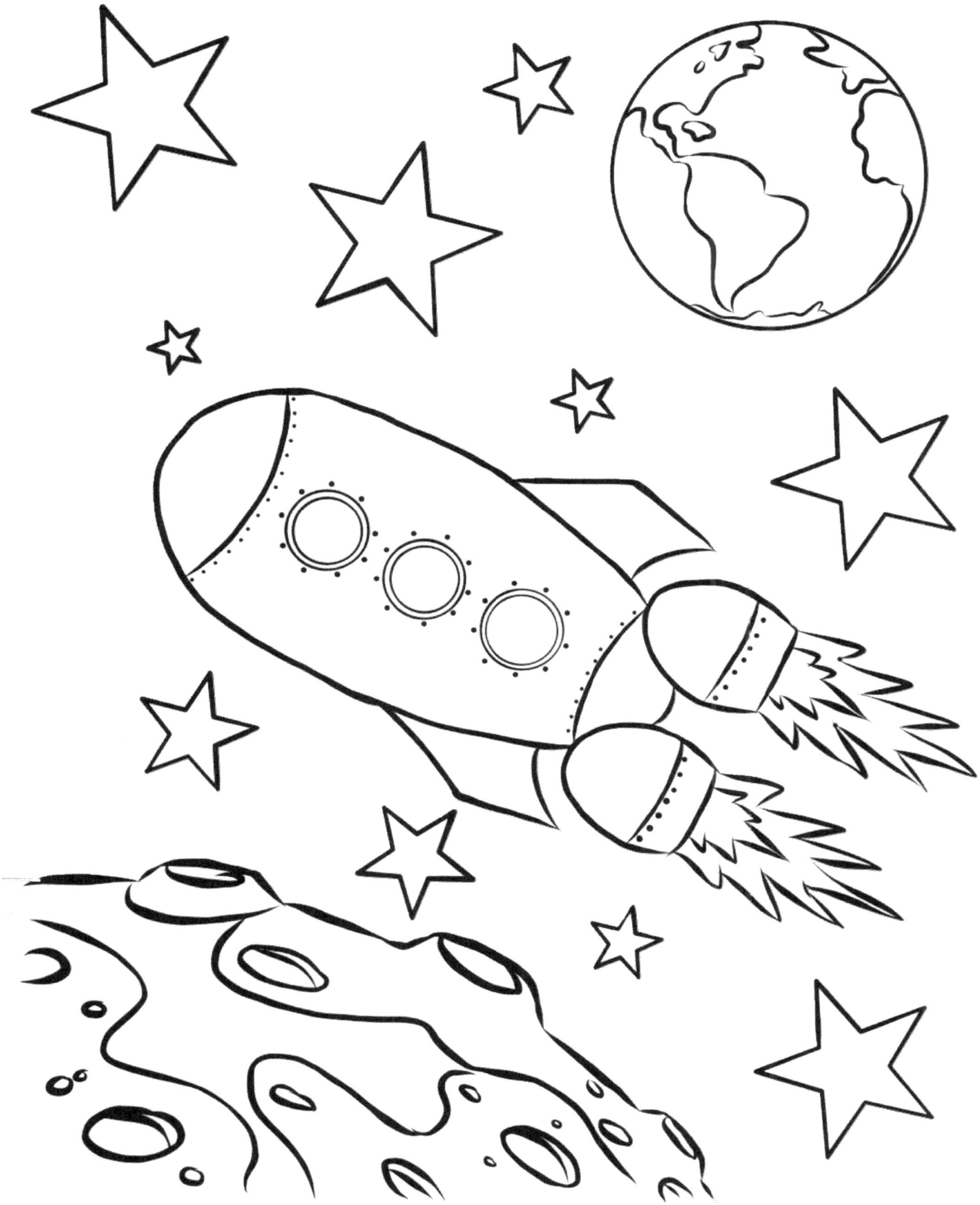

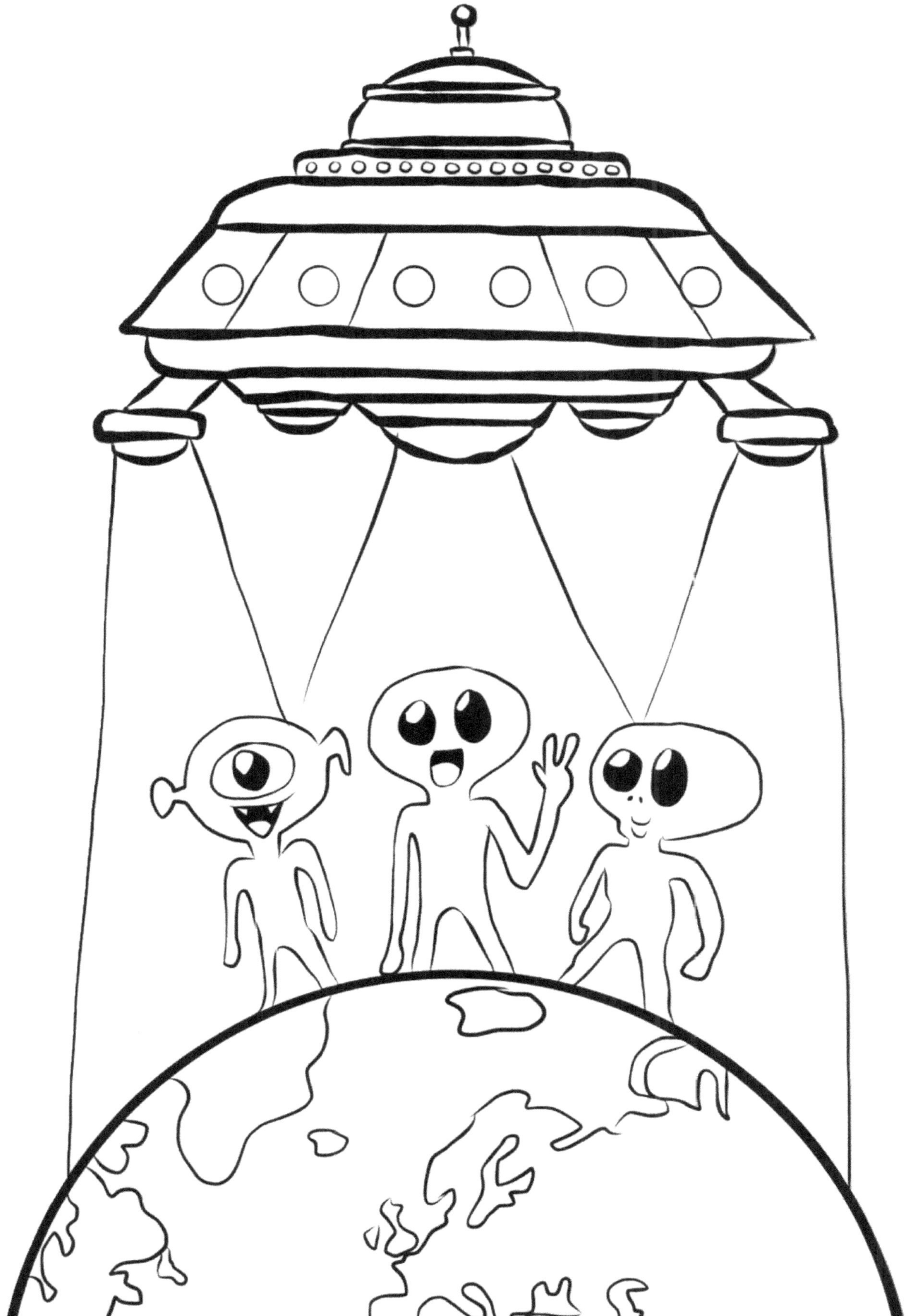

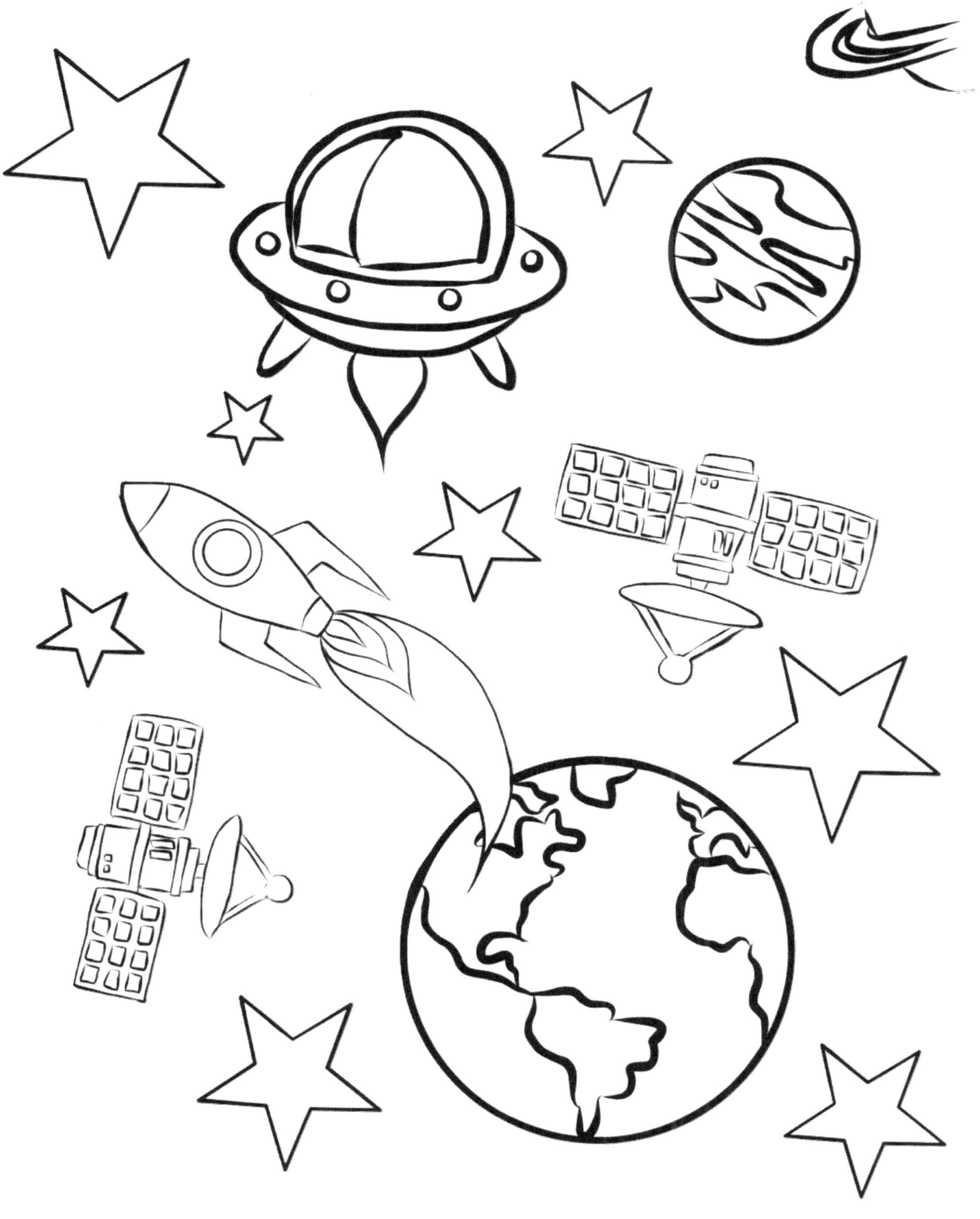

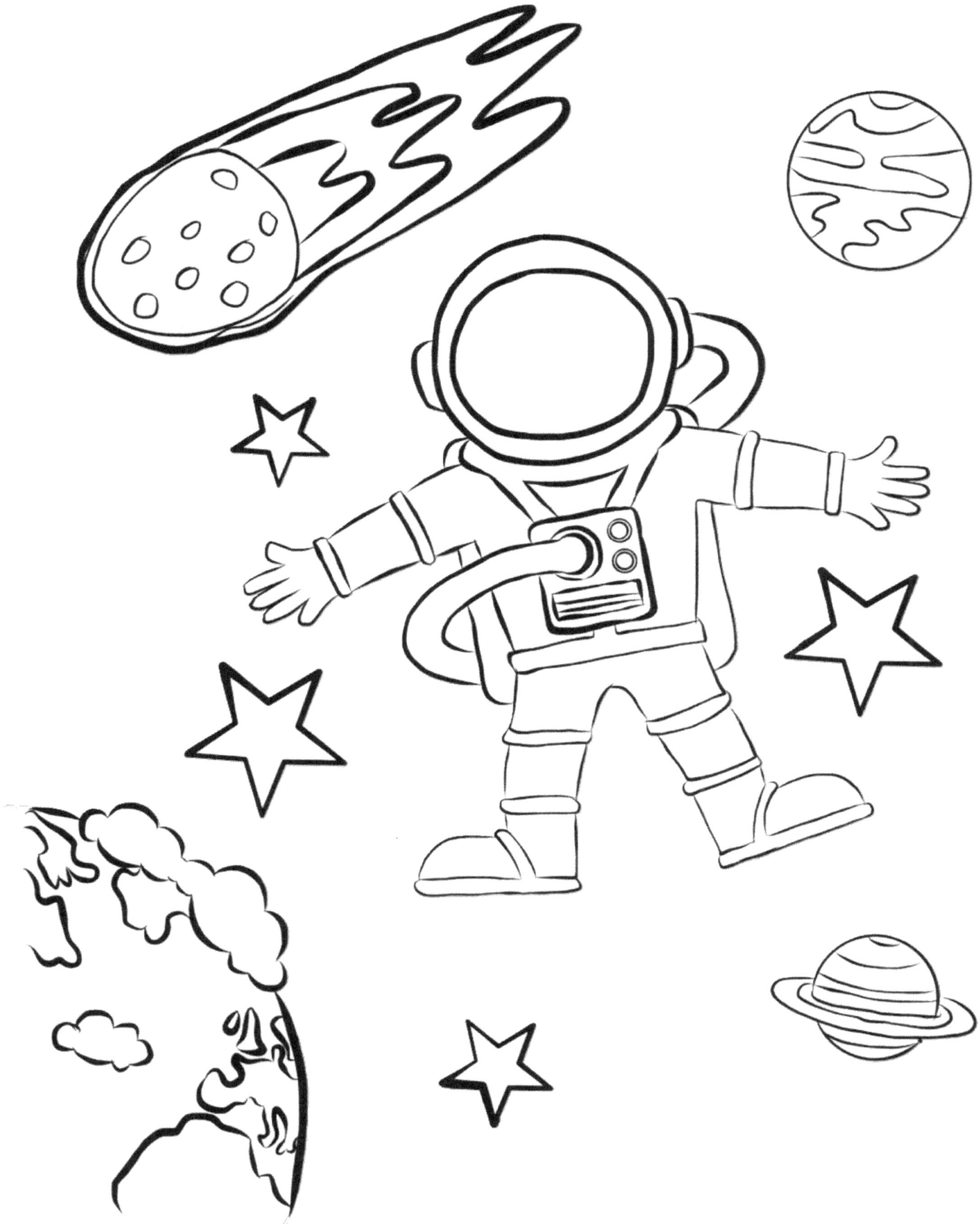

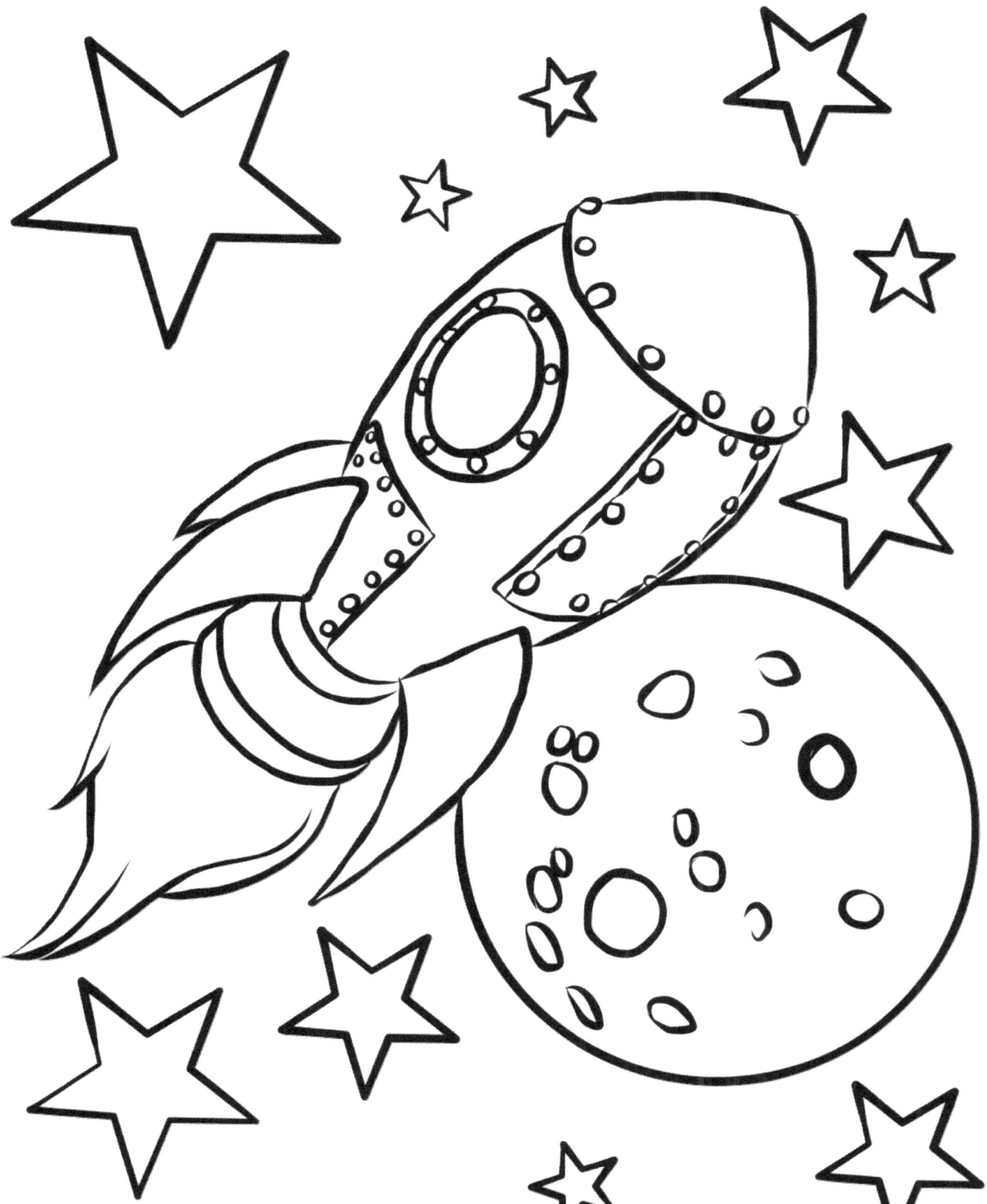

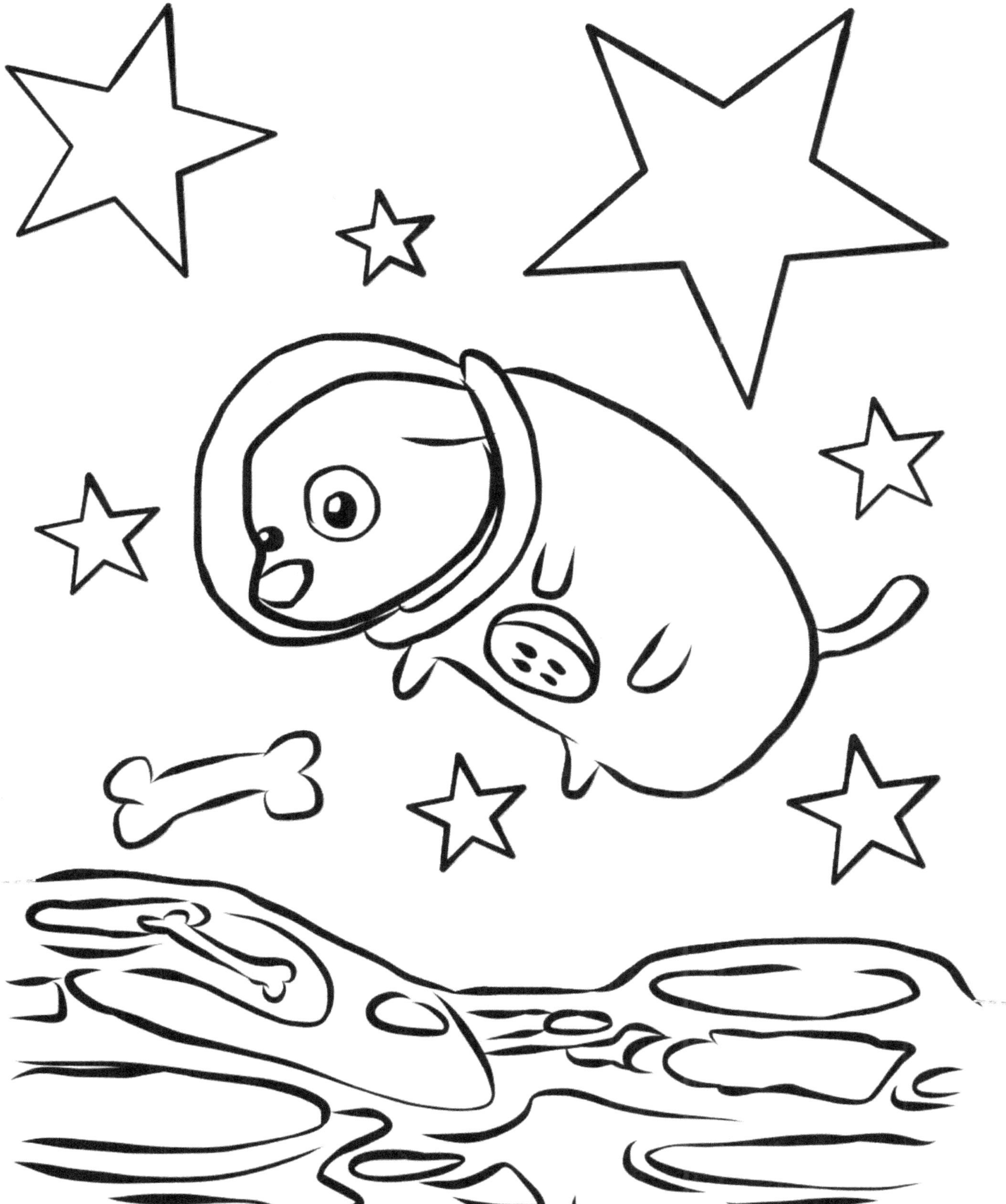

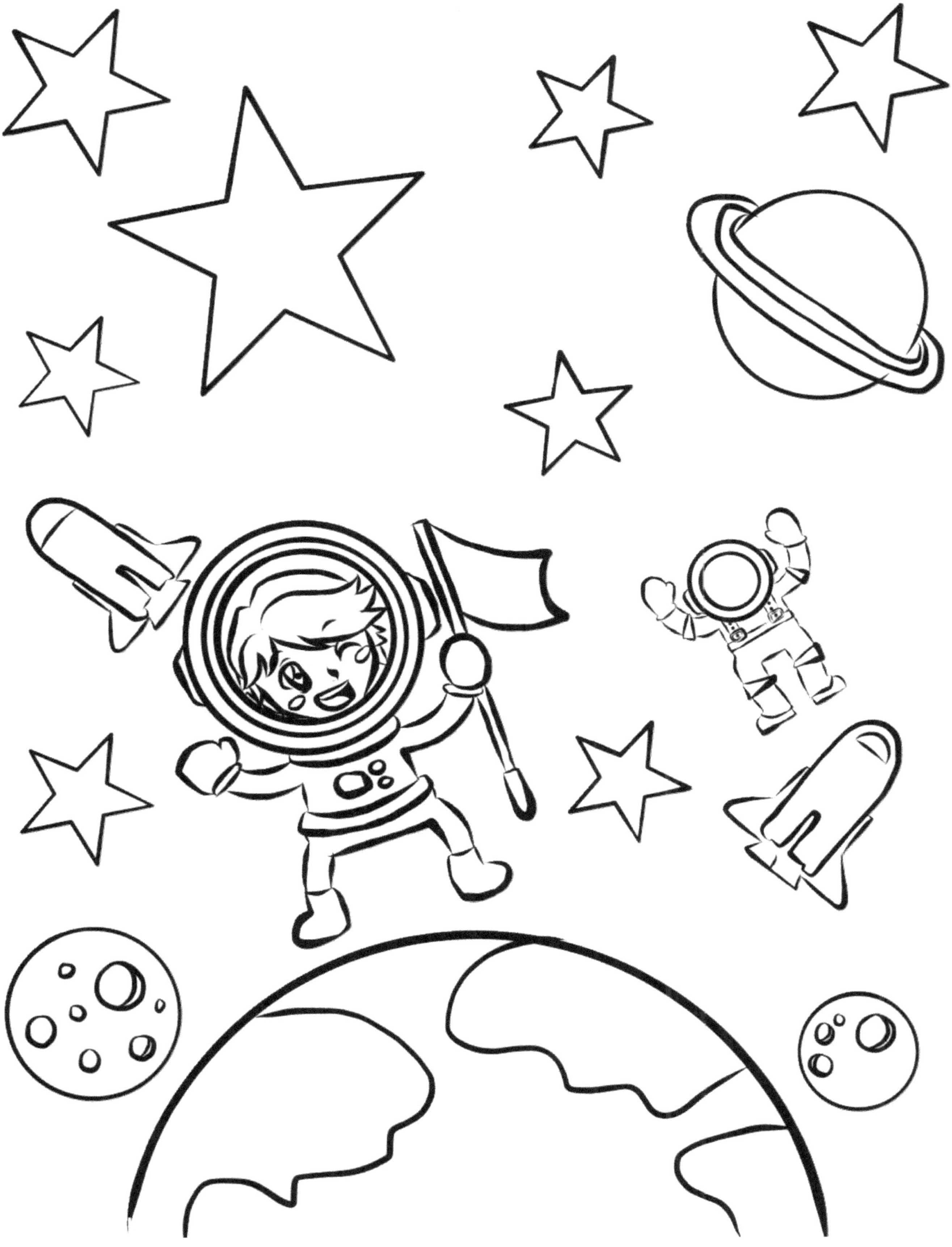

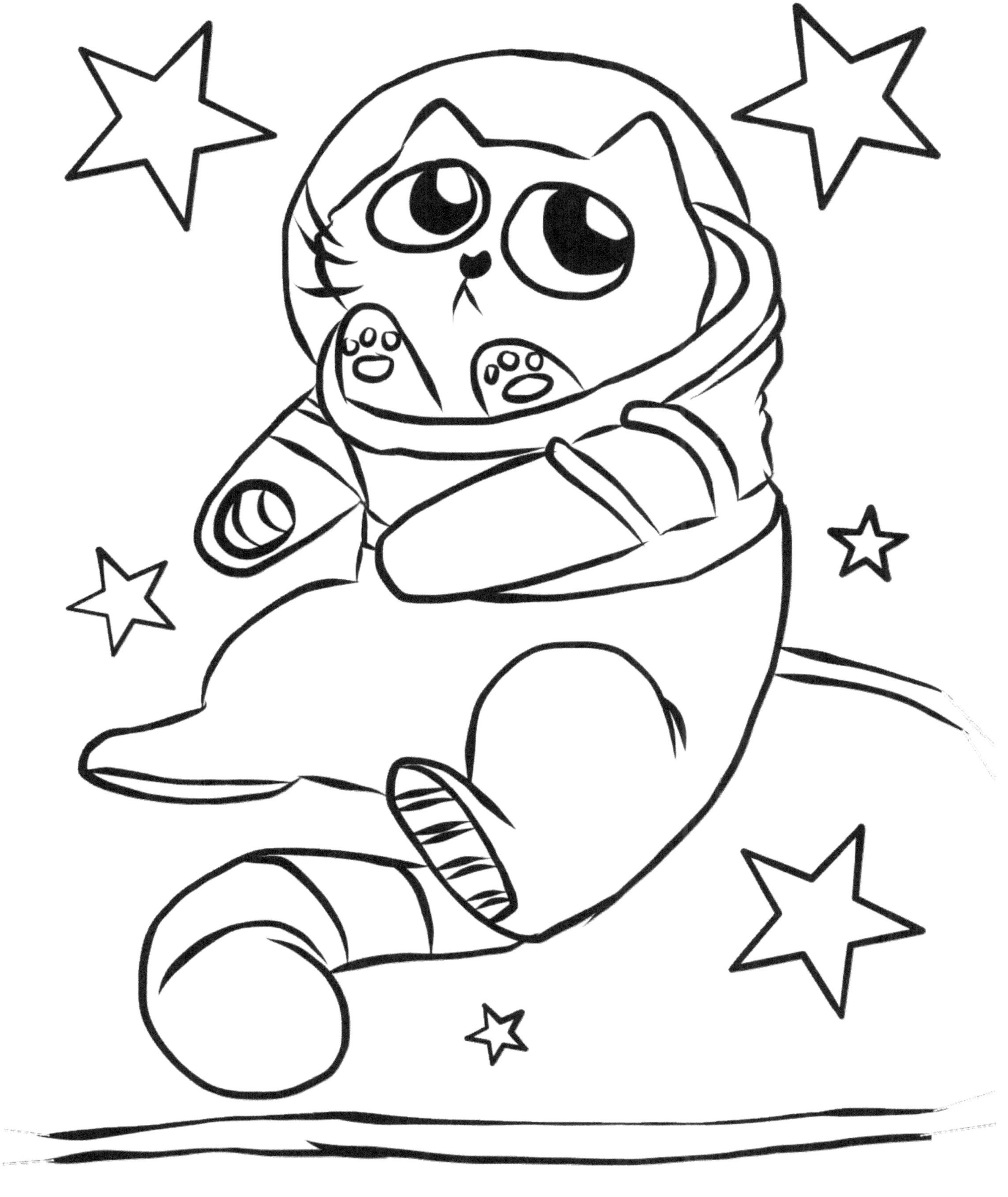

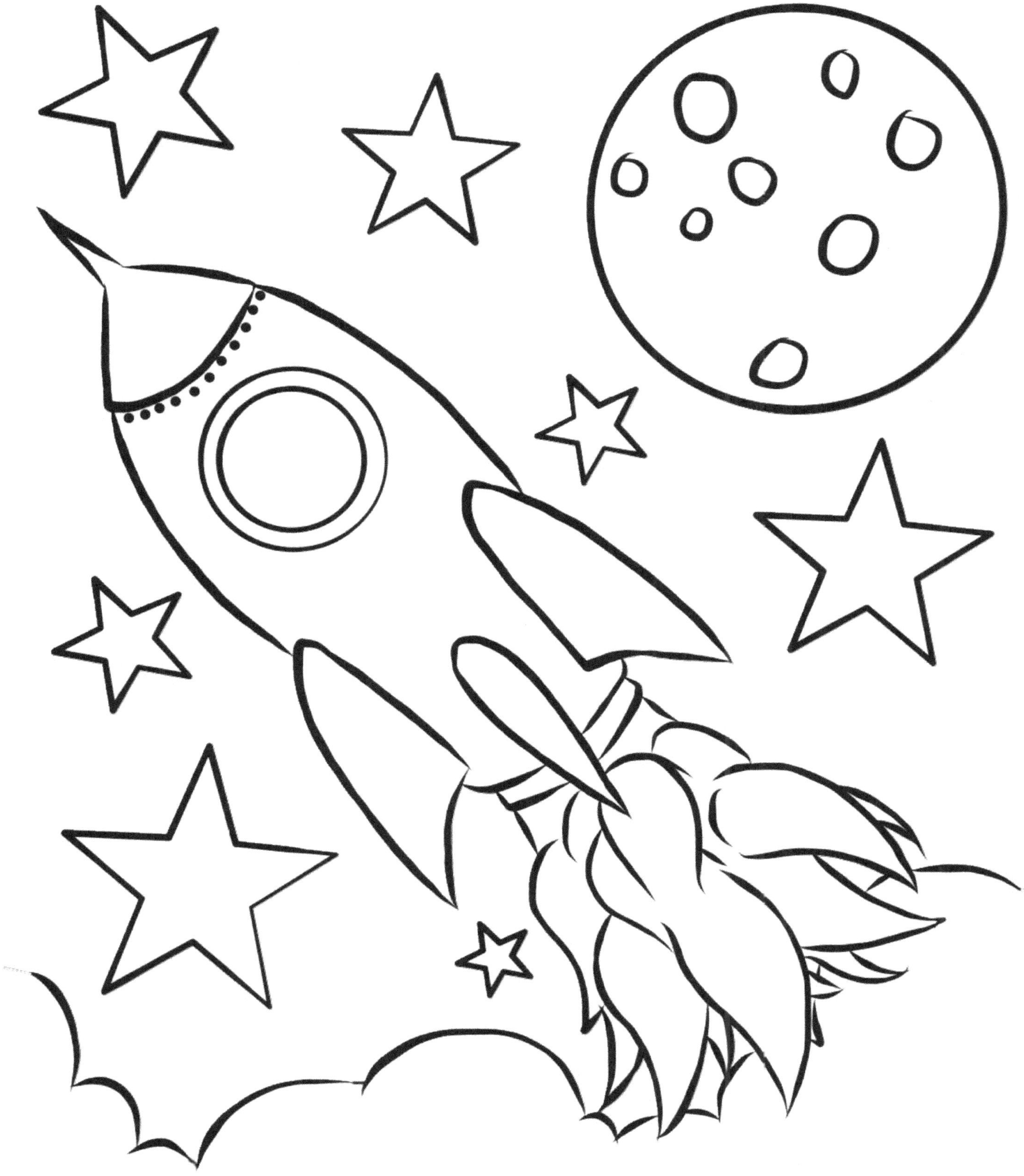

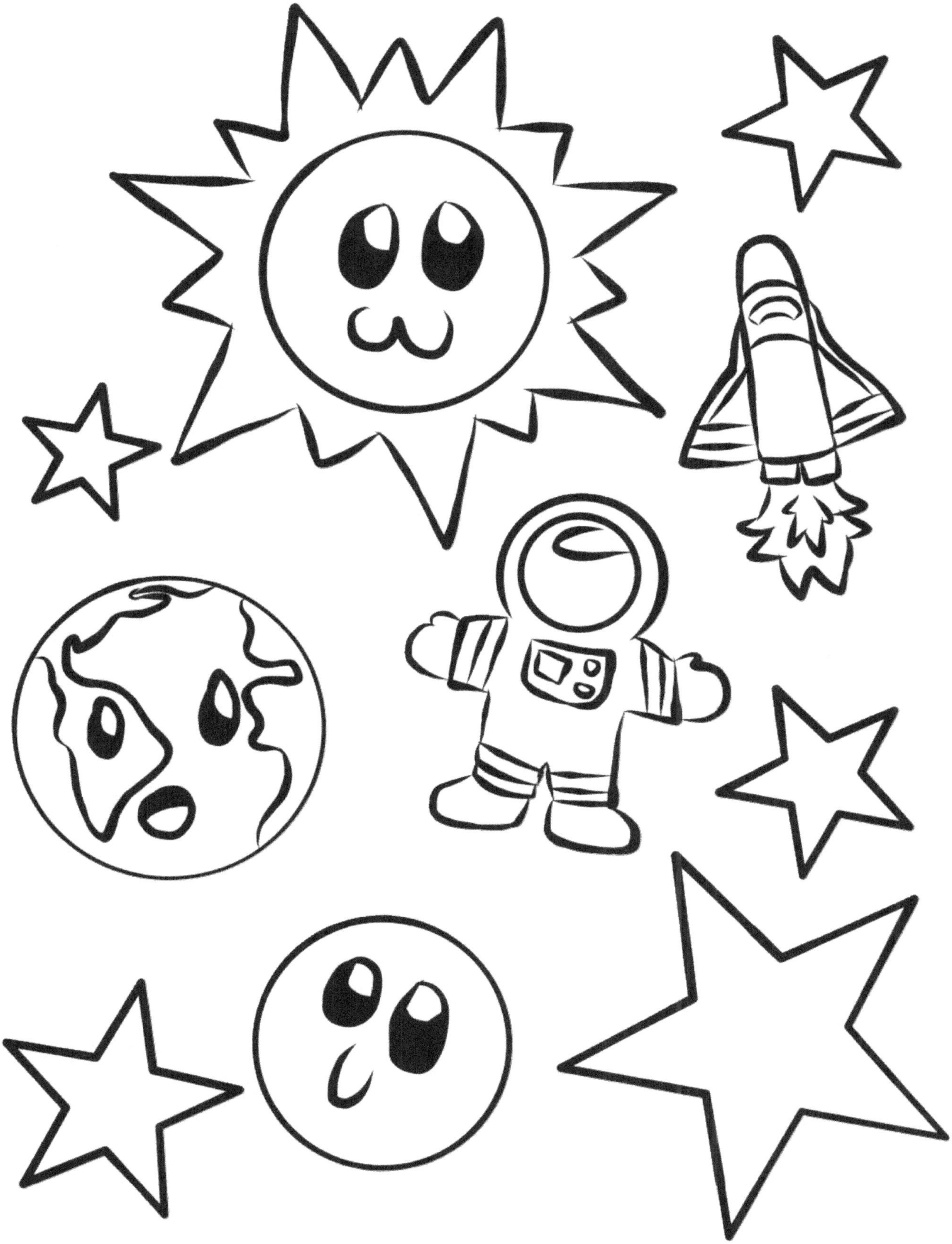

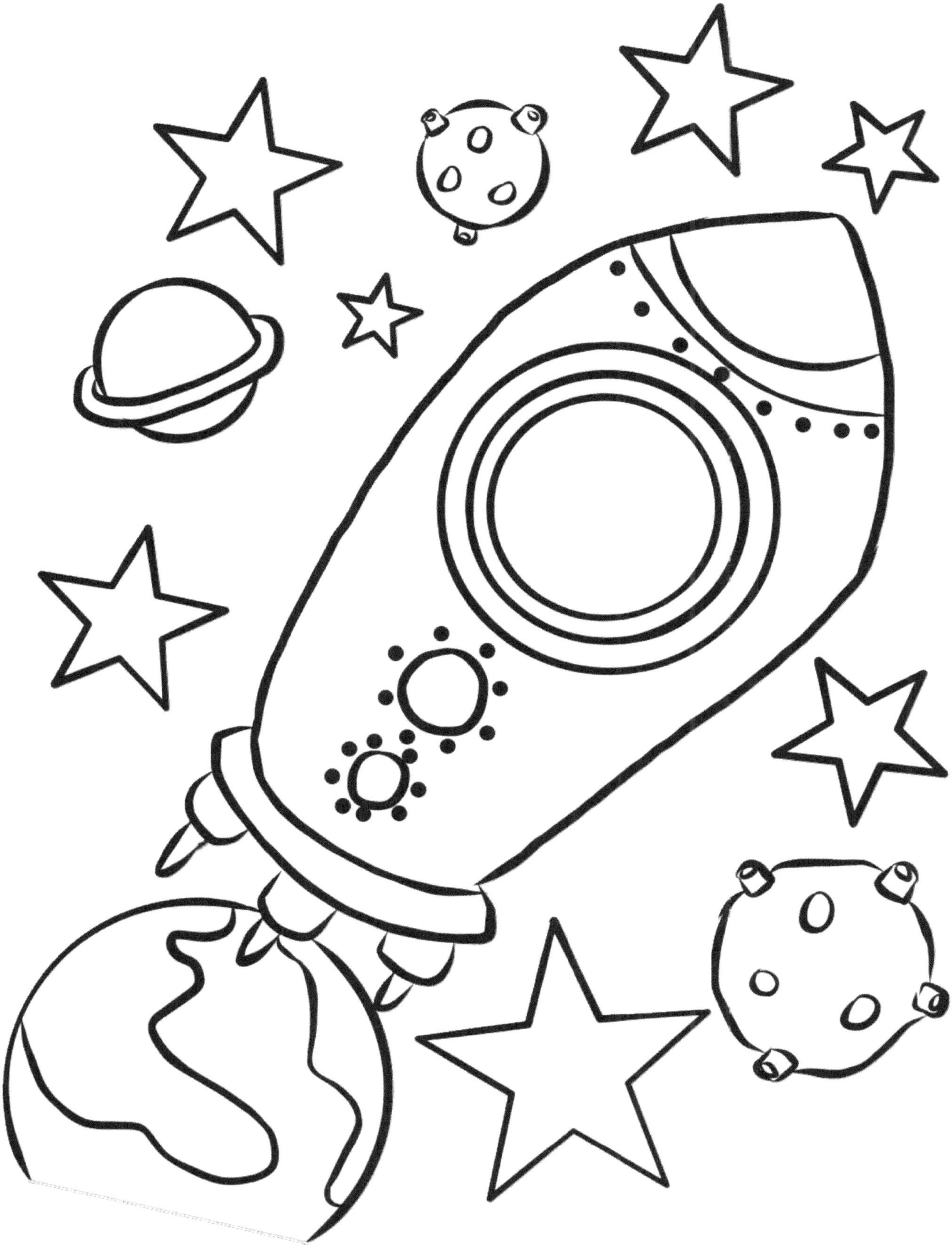

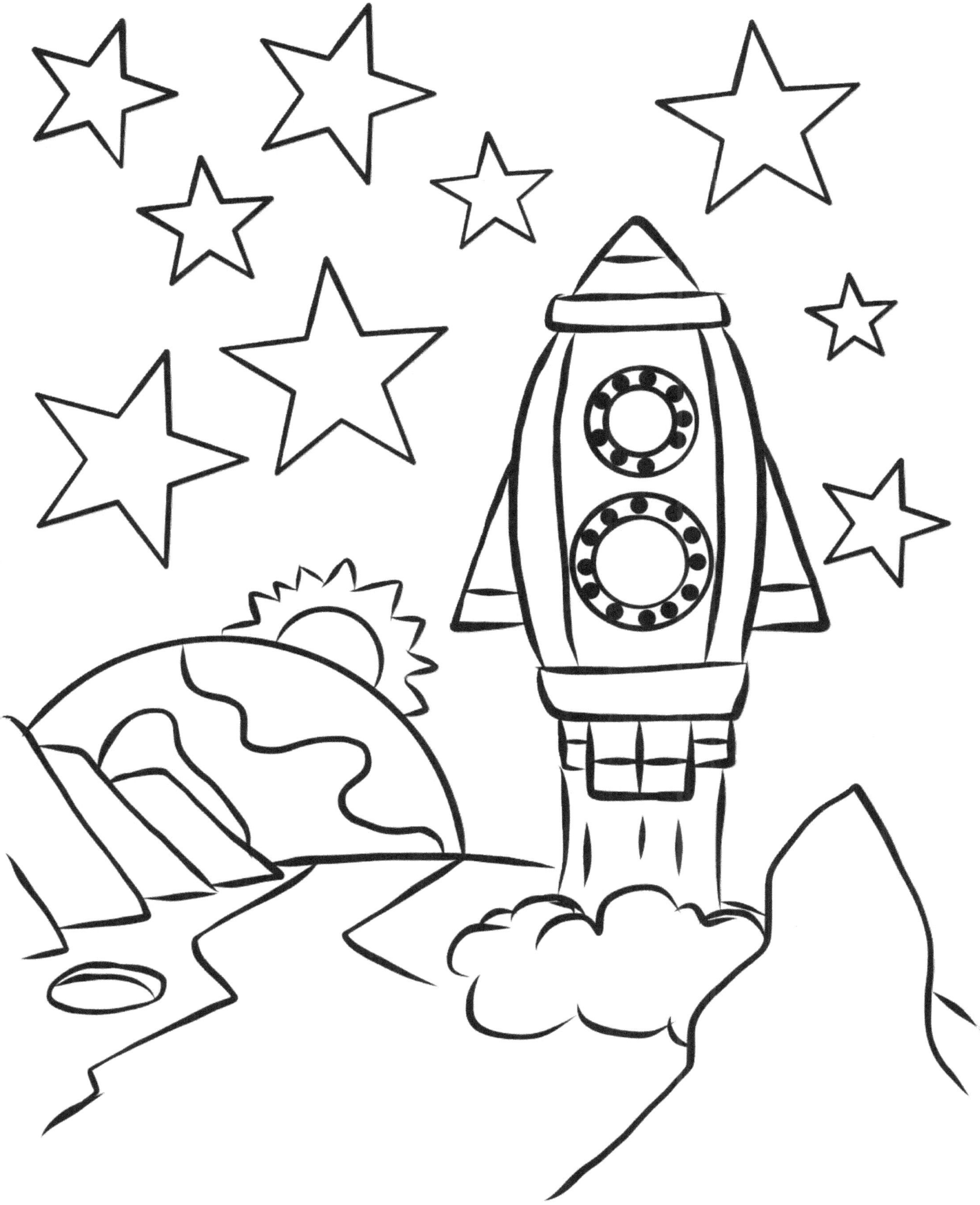

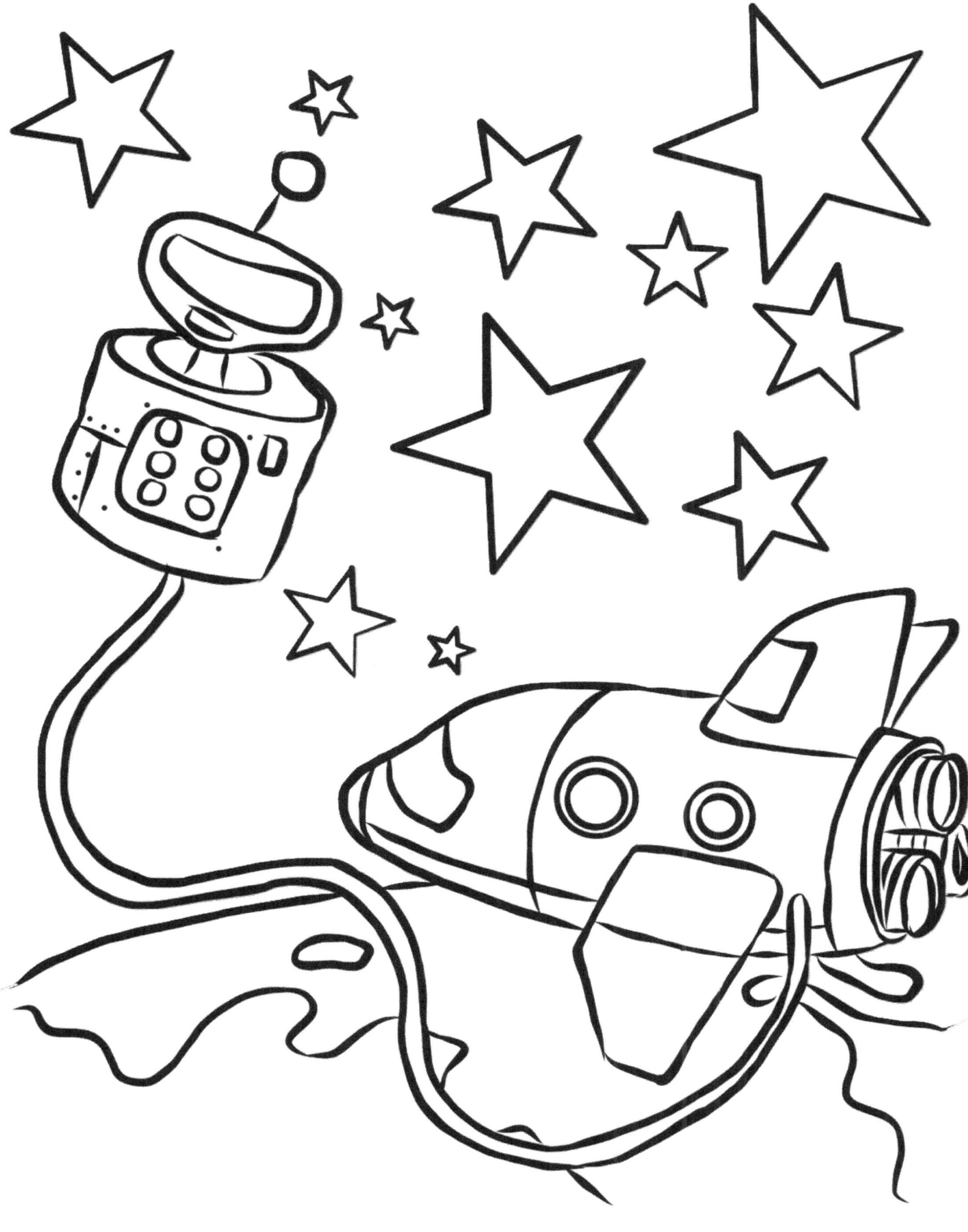

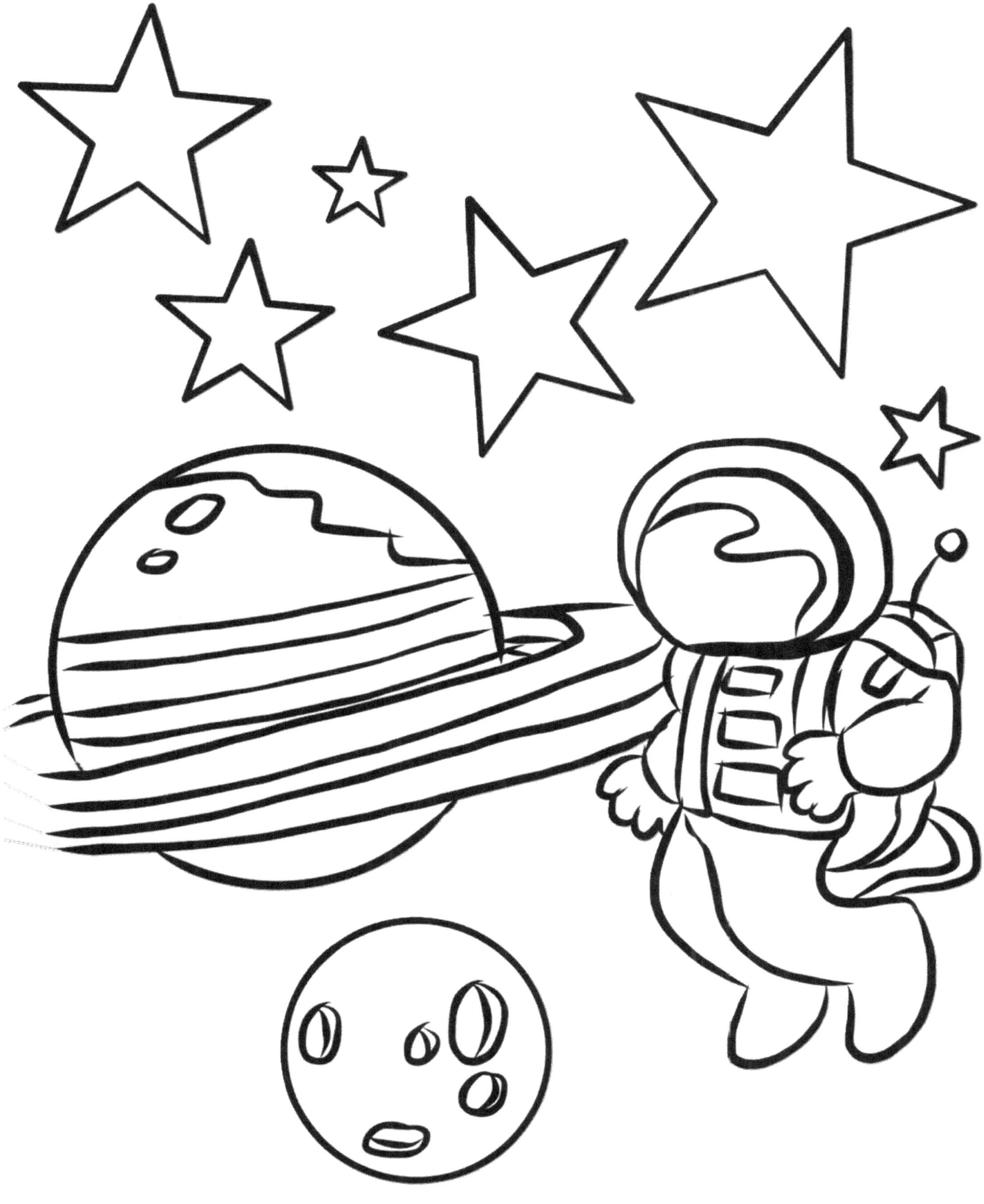

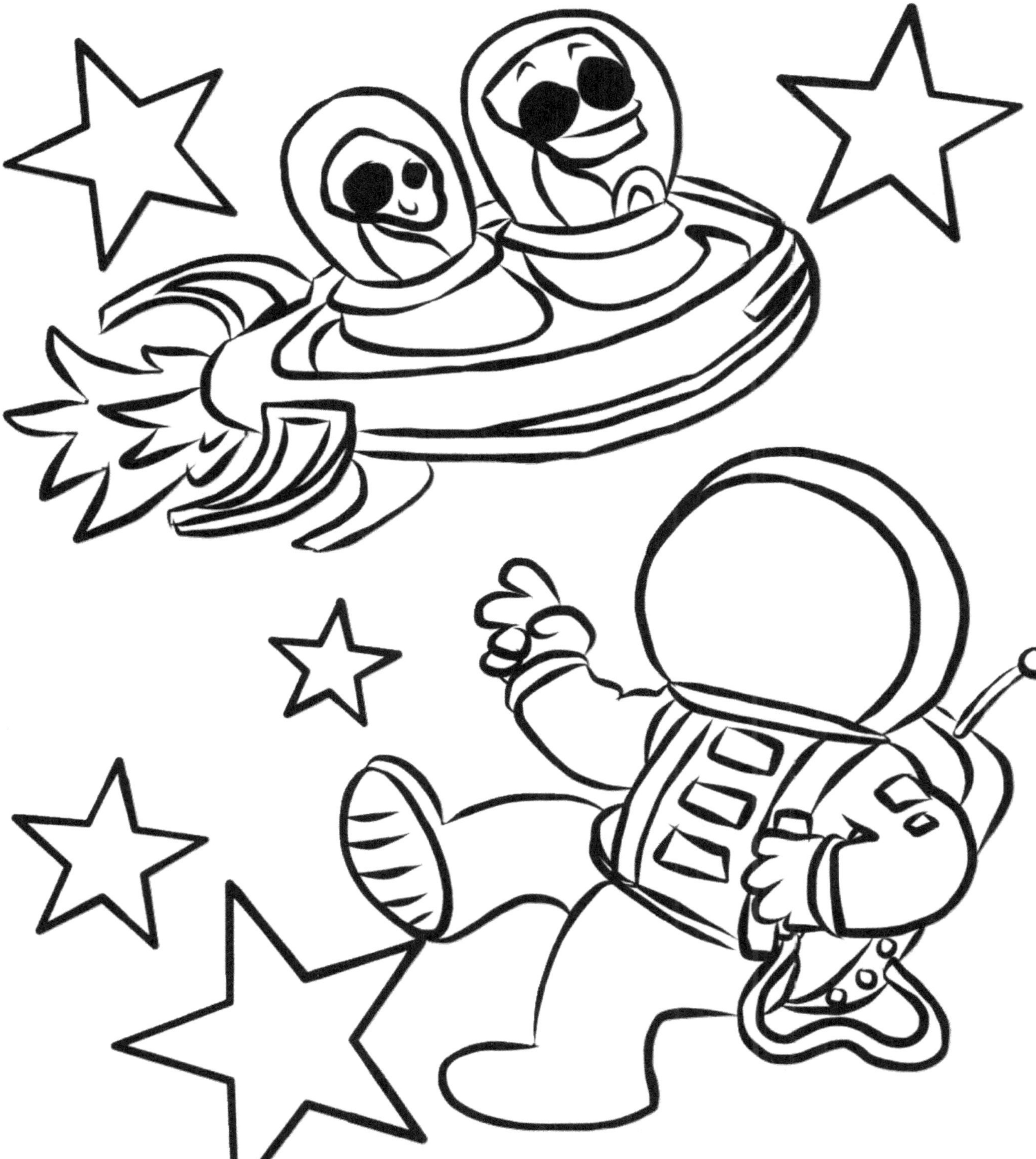

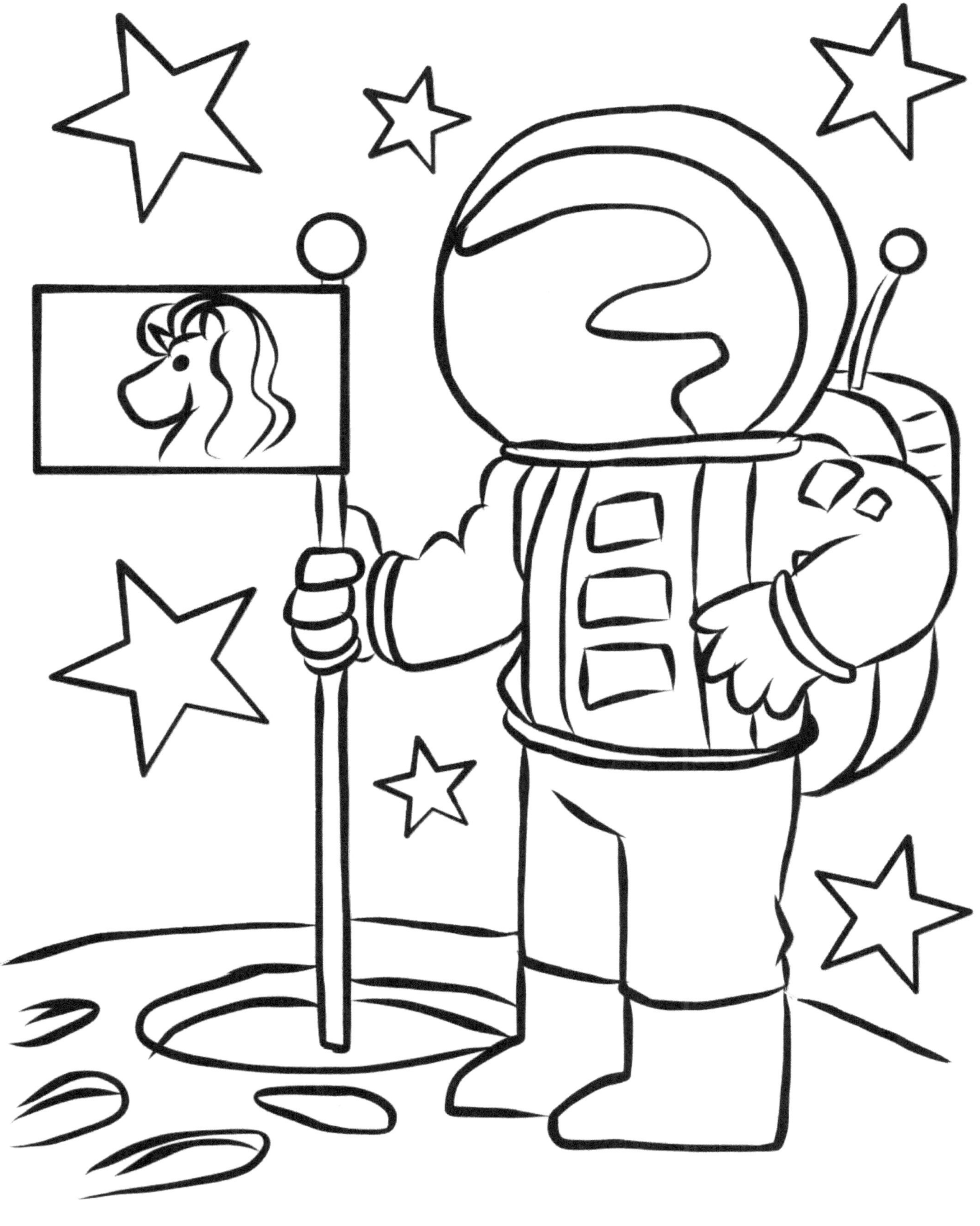

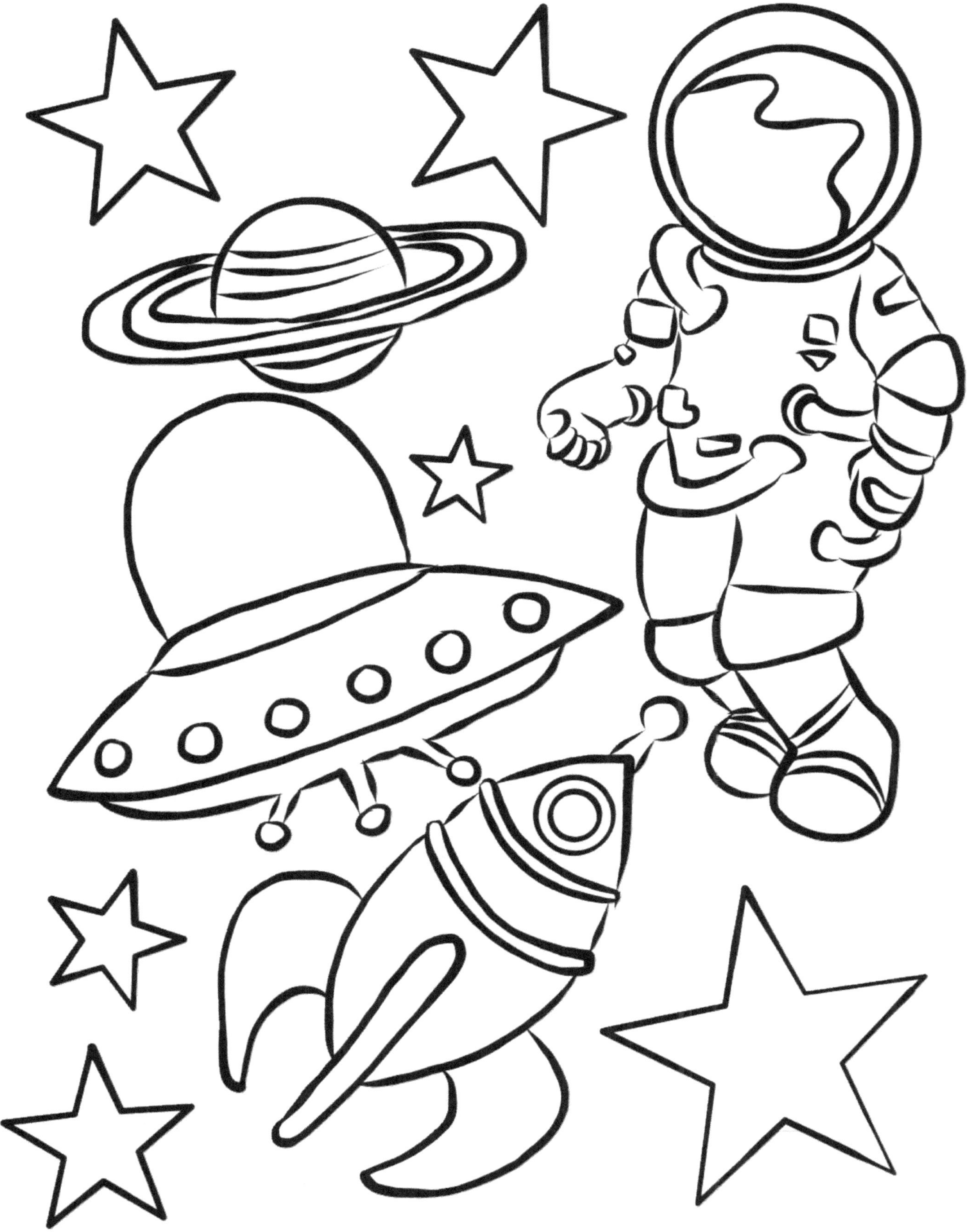

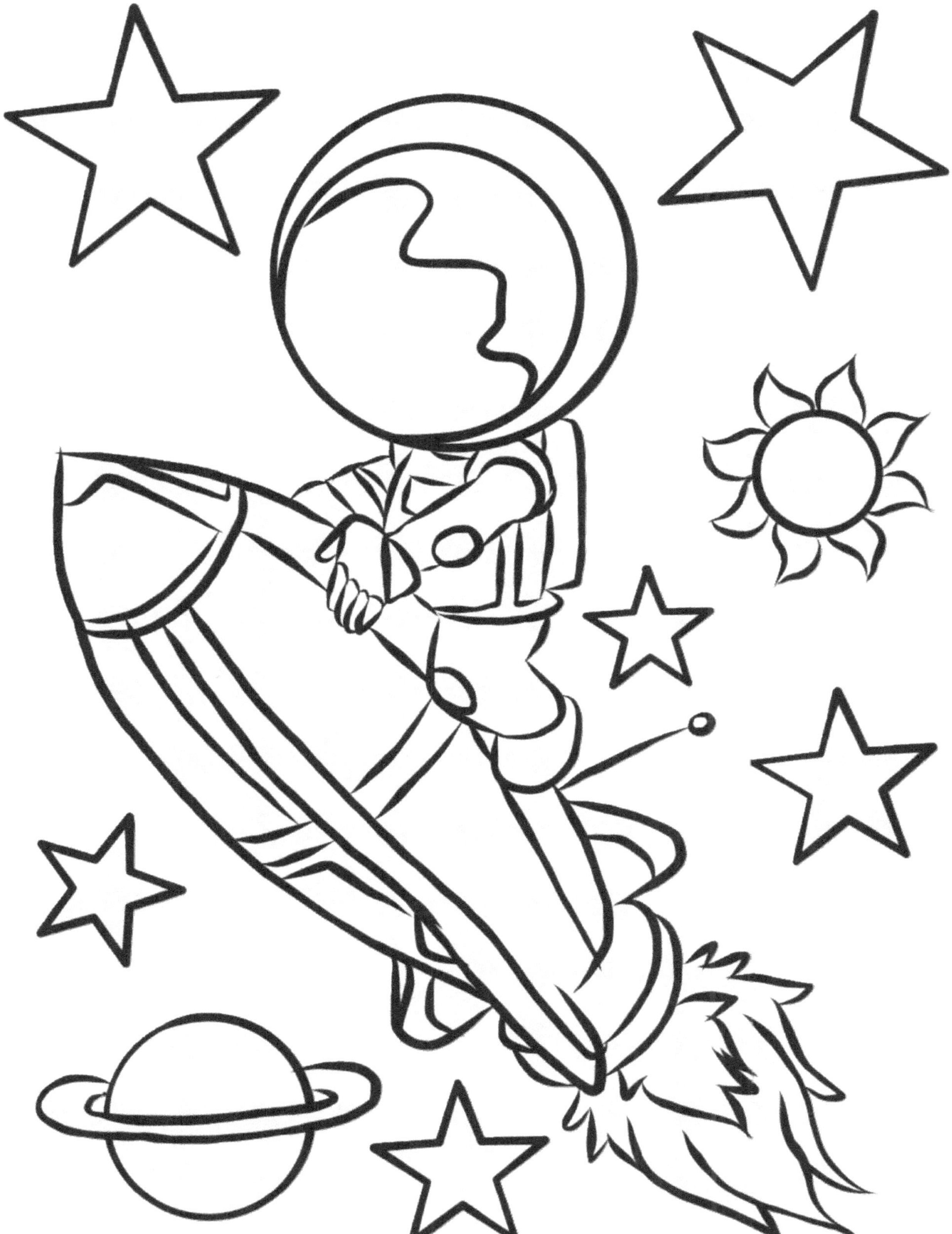

www.ingramcontent.com/pod-product-compliance
Lightning Source LLC
Chambersburg PA
CBHW081633220526
45468CB00009B/2414
* 9 7 8 1 9 8 3 4 1 0 6 2 8 *